4

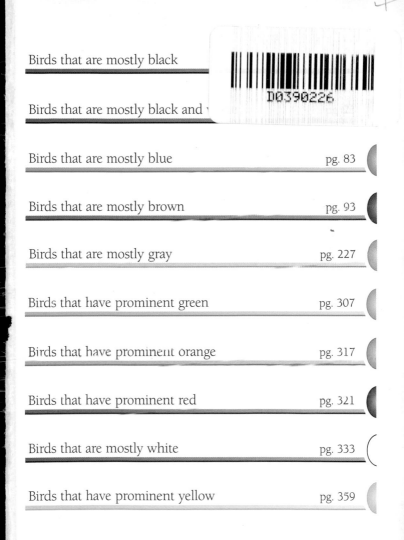

Birds of Alaska

Field Guide

by Stan Tekiela

Adventure Publications, Inc.
Cambridge, Minnesota

To my wife Katherine and daughter Abigail with all my love
Acknowledgments

Special thanks to the National Wildlife Refuge System, which stewards the land that is critical to many bird species. Thanks also to Thede Tobish for reviewing the range maps.

Edited by Sandy Livoti and Deborah Walsh
Book design and illustrations by Jonathan Norberg
Range maps produced by Anthony Hertzel

Photo credits by photographer and page number:
Cover photo: Bald Eagle by Stan Tekiela
Mike Danzenbaker: 12, 18 (drying), 240 (female) **Dudley Edmondson**: 16 (perching), 60, 70, 96, 102, 116, 132, 142, 146 (female, in flight), 186, 210 (soaring), 214 (both perching juveniles), 262, 280 (perching, both soaring), 290 (perching, in flight), 294 (perching, juvenile), 296 (juvenile), 340 (breeding, in flight), 342 (breeding), 344 (both), 356 (swimming) **B. Gerlach/DPA***: 316 (male) **Kevin T. Karlson**: 42, 162 (female), 248, 270 **Gary Kramer**: 74, 196, 220 **Greg Lasley/KAC Productions**: 338 **Bill Marchel**: 90 (male), 124 (red morph), 354 (in flight) **Maslowski Productions**: 98, 124 (Pacific), 154 (breeding female), 226, 228, 306 (male), 318 (male) 320, 334 (winter), 366 **Anthony Mercieca/DPA***: 316 (female) **Steve Mortensen**: 66, 84, 108 (both), 194 **Warren Nelson**: 362 (female) **Johann Schumacher/CLO***: 90 (female) **Brian E. Small**: 18 (swimming), 22 (both), 24 (all), 28 (both), 32 (female), 44, 46, 48, 54 (male, female), 56 (breeding), 58 (both), 64, 68 (male), 88, 92, 100, 118 (non-breeding male), 122 (non-breeding), 128 (pale morph), 130 (non-breeding), 138, 148 (both), 152 (both breeding), 160, 184, 188, 192, 200, 218, 224 (perching), 244, 252, 254 (non-breeding male), 306 (female), 318 (female), 328, 332 (in flight), 336, 340 (non-breeding), 342 (winter), 346 (winter), 348 (all), 350 (all), 358 (female), 360 **Stan Tekiela**: 2 (both), 4, 6, 8, 10, 14, 16 (in flight), 20 (all), 26 (both), 30 (both), 32 (male), 34, 36 (breeding), 38, 40 (both breeding), 50, 52, 56 (winter), 62, 72 (both), 78 (both), 80 (all), 82, 86 (both), 94 (male, female), 104, 106, 110 (both), 112, 114, 118 (male, female), 120 (both), 122 (breeding), 126, 128 (bottom), 130 (breeding), 136, 140, 144, 146 (male), 150, 154 (breeding male), 156 (both breeding), 158, 162 (male), 164 (both), 168 (both), 170, 172, 174 (both), 176 (both), 178 (both), 180, 182, 190 (both), 202, 204, 206 (both), 208, 214 (perching light morph), 216, 222, 230, 232, 234, 236, 238 (all), 240 (male), 242 (both), 246, 250, 254 (male, female), 256, 258, 260, 264 (both), 266, 268 (both), 272, 276, 278, 280 (juvenile), 282, 284 (both), 286 perching, 288, 292 (soaring), 294 (in flight), 296 (perching, soaring juvenile), 298 (breeding), 300 (both), 302 (both), 304 (all), 308, 310, 312, 314 (male, in flight), 322, 324, 330 (female, in flight), 332 (perching, juvenile), 342 (in flight), 346 (breeding, in flight, juvenile), 352 (all), 354 (swimming, juvenile), 356 (in flight, juvenile), 358 (male) 362 (male) 368 **Brian K. Wheeler**: 146 (both juveniles), 210 (female, in flight), 212 (all), 214 (perching dark morph, all soaring), 224 (soaring, both juveniles), 290 (both juveniles), 292 (male), 296 (soaring) **Jim Zipp**: 36 (non-breeding), 54 (winter male, in flight), 68 (in flight), 76 (both), 94 (Hoary), 134, 166, 198, 210 (soaring juvenile), 274, 286 (in flight), 298 (winter), 326, 364
*DPA: Dembinsky Photo Associates; CLO: Cornell Laboratory of Ornithology
To the best of the publisher's knowledge, all photos were of live birds.

ISBN-13: 978-1-59193-096-9
ISBN-10: 1-59193-096-0

TABLE OF CONTENTS
Introduction

WHY WATCH BIRDS IN ALASKA?

Millions of people have discovered bird feeding. It's a simple and enjoyable way to bring the beauty of birds closer to your home. Watching birds at your feeder often leads to a lifetime pursuit of bird identification. The *Birds of Alaska Field Guide* is for those who want to identify the common birds of Alaska.

There are over 800 species of birds found in North America. In Alaska alone there have been more than 400 different kinds of birds recorded throughout the years. These bird sightings were diligently recorded by hundreds of bird watchers and became part of the official state record. From these valuable records, I have chosen 150 of the most common and easily seen birds of Alaska to include in this field guide.

Bird watching, or birding, is the most popular spectator sport in America. Its appeal in Alaska is due, in part, to an unusually rich and abundant birdlife. Why are there so many birds? One reason is open space. With more than 571,000 square miles (1,484,600 sq. km), Alaska is about one-fifth the size of the continental U.S. and is our largest state From its farthest point east to its farthest point west, Alaska covers almost 2,400 miles (3,865 km), a distance greater than New York to San Francisco. Even if you were to divide Alaska in two, it would still rank first and second in size, with Texas coming in third. Alaska's total population, however, is only about 648,000 people. While this averages to just one person per square mile, most are located in four major cities in southern Alaska.

Open space is not the only reason there is such an abundance of birds in Alaska. It's also the diversity of habitat. Alaska has several mountain ranges–the Coast Range (includes the Kenai, Chugach, Kodiak and Saint Elias Ranges), the Alaska Aleutian Range and Brooks Range. These ranges have 19 peaks higher than 14,000 feet (4,250 m), with Mount McKinley reaching 20,320 feet (6,200 m). Mountainous regions are good places to see Boreal Chickadees and White-winged Crossbills.

Besides mountains, Alaska has over 5,000 glaciers–this is more than half of all glaciers in the world. It also has lush rain forests on the southern coast and dry sand dunes in the Arctic Circle.

Alaska has almost 45,000 square miles (117,000 sq. km) of tidal shoreline. Some areas have the greatest tidal variations in the world–up to 30 feet (9 m). The coastline of Alaska is longer than the coasts of all lower 48 states combined. It includes the Aleutian Island chain, which is at least 1,000 miles (1,610 km) in length. Coasts are great places to see birds such as Common Eiders and Common Murres.

Fresh water also plays a large part in Alaska's bird populations. About three million lakes in the state are over 2 acres (.8 ha). Small lakes are wonderful places to see Red-necked Phalaropes and other birds. The largest lake, Lake Illiamna, covers around 1,000 square miles (2,600 sq. km). The Yukon River, the third longest river in the U.S., flows over 1,800 miles (2,900 km). Most rivers in Alaska are great places to see waterfowl such as Harlequin Ducks. It's always worth time to investigate bodies of water in Alaska for the presence of birds.

Varying habitats in Alaska also mean variations in the weather. Alaska's record temperatures range from a high of 100 °F (38° C) to a low of -80° F (-62° C). Rainfall ranges from 2 inches (5 cm) annually in parts of the Arctic to over 300 inches (762 cm) in the rain forests of the southern coast. The weather is as diverse as the habitats in Alaska, making it one of the best places to see a wide variety of birds.

Wherever you go in Alaska, no matter if you're in the dry arctic tundra or moist mountains in southern parts of the state, there are birds to watch every season of the year. Whether witnessing the migration of hawks in fall or welcoming back shorebirds in spring, there is variety and excitement in birding as each season turns to the next.

OBSERVE WITH A STRATEGY;
TIPS FOR IDENTIFYING BIRDS

Identifying birds isn't as difficult as you might think. By simply following a few basic strategies, you can increase your chances of successfully identifying most birds you see! One of the first and easiest things to do when you see a new bird is to note its color. (Also, since this book is organized by color, you will go right to that color section to find it.)

Next, note the size of the bird. A strategy to quickly estimate size is to select a small-, medium- and large-sized bird to use for reference. For example, most people are familiar with robins. A robin, measured from tip of the bill to tip of the tail, is 10 inches (25 cm) long. Using the robin as an example of a medium-sized bird, select two other birds, one smaller and one larger. Many people use an American Tree Sparrow, about 6 inches (15 cm), and a Northwestern Crow, about 18 inches (45 cm). When you see a bird that you don't know, you can quickly ask yourself, "Is it smaller than a robin, but larger than a sparrow?" When you look in your field guide to help identify your bird, you'll know it's roughly between 6-10 inches (15-25 cm) long. This will help to narrow your choices.

Next, note the size, shape and color of the bill. Is it long, short, thick, thin, pointed, blunt, curved or straight? Seed-eating birds have bills that are thick and strong enough to crack even the toughest seeds. Birds that sip nectar such as Rufous Hummingbirds need long thin bills to reach deep into flowers. Hawks and owls tear their prey with very sharp, curving bills. Sometimes, just noting the bill shape can help you decide whether the bird is a woodpecker, sparrow, grosbeak, blackbird or bird of prey.

Next, take a look around and note the habitat in which you see the bird. Is it wading in a saltwater marsh? Walking along a riverbank or on the beach? Soaring in the sky? Is it perched high in the trees or hopping along the forest floor? Because of their preferences in diet and habitat, you'll usually see robins hopping on the ground, but not often eating seeds at a feeder.

Noticing what a bird is eating will give you another clue to help you identify that bird. Feeding is a big part of any bird's life. Fully one-third of all bird activity revolves around searching for and catching food, or actually eating. While birds don't always follow all the rules of what we think they eat, you can make some general assumptions. Northern Flickers, for instance, feed upon ants and other insects, so you wouldn't expect to see them visiting a backyard feeder. Some birds such as Tree Swallows and Cliff Swallows feed upon flying insects and spend hours swooping and diving to catch a meal.

Sometimes you can identify a bird by the way it perches. Body posture can help you tell the difference between a Northwestern Crow and Red-tailed Hawk. Crows lean forward over their feet on a branch, while hawks perch in a vertical position. Look for this the next time you see a large unidentified bird in a tree.

Birds in flight are often difficult to identify, but noting the size and shape of the wing will help. A bird's wing size is in direct proportion to its body size, weight and type of flying. The shape of the wing determines if the bird flies fast and with precision, or slowly and less precisely. Birds such as Ruby-crowned Kinglets, which flit around in thick tangles of branches, have short round wings. Birds that soar on warm updrafts of air, such as Rough-legged Hawks, have long broad wings. Barn Swallows have short pointed wings that slice through the air, propelling their swift and accurate flight.

Some birds have unique flight patterns that aid in identification. The Northwestern Crow flies with constantly flapping wings, while the Common Raven soars on outstretched wings. Taking note of differences such as these can really help differentiate between similar-looking birds.

While it's not easy to make these observations in the short time you often have to watch a "mystery bird," practicing these methods of identification will greatly expand your skills in birding. Also, seek the guidance of a more experienced birder who will help you improve your skills and answer questions on the spot.

BIRD BASICS

It's easier to identify birds and communicate about them if you know the names of the different parts of a bird. For instance, it's more effective to use the word "crest" to indicate the set of extra long feathers on top of the head of a Steller's Jay than to try to describe it.

The following illustration points out the basic parts of a bird. Because it is a composite of many birds, it shouldn't be confused with any actual bird.

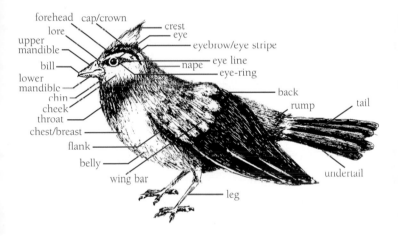

Bird Color Variables

No other animal has a color palette like a bird's. Brilliant blues, lemon yellows, showy reds and iridescent greens are common-place within the bird world. In general, the male birds are more colorful than their female counterparts. This is probably to help the male attract a mate, essentially saying, "Hey, look at me!" It also calls attention to the male's overall health. The better the condition of his feathers, the better his food source and territory, and therefore the better his potential for a mate.

Female birds that don't look like their male counterparts (such species are called sexually dimorphic, meaning "two forms") are often a nondescript color, as seen with the White-winged Crossbill. The muted tones help hide the females during weeks of motionless incubation, and draw less attention to them when they are out feeding or taking a break from the rigors of raising their young.

In some species such as the Bald Eagle, Steller's Jay and Downy Woodpecker, male birds look nearly identical to the females. In the case of woodpeckers, the sexes are differentiated only by a single red mark or sometimes yellow mark. Depending upon the species, the mark may be on top of the head, face, nape of neck or just behind the bill.

During the first year, juvenile birds often look like the mothers. Since brightly colored feathers are used mainly for attracting a mate, young non-breeding males don't have a need for colorful plumage. It is not until the first spring molt (or several years later, depending on the species) that young males obtain their breeding colors.

Both breeding and winter plumages are the result of molting. Molting is the process of dropping old worn feathers and replacing them with new ones. All birds molt, typically twice a year, with the spring molt usually occurring in late winter. During this time, most birds produce their breeding plumage (brighter colors for attracting mates), which lasts throughout the summer.

Winter plumage is the result of the late summer molt, which serves a couple of important functions. First, it adds feathers for warmth in the coming winter. Second, in some species it produces feathers that tend to be drab in color, which helps to camouflage the birds and hide them from predators. The winter plumage of the male Common Loon, for example, is shades of gray unlike its bold black-and-white pattern in summer. Luckily for us, some birds such as the Steller's Jay retain their bright summer colors all year long.

Bird Nests

Bird nests are truly an amazing feat of engineering. Imagine building your home strong enough to weather a storm, large enough to hold your entire family, insulated enough to shelter them from cold and heat, and waterproof enough to keep out rain. Now, build it without any blueprints or directions, and without the use of your hands or feet! Birds do!

Before building a nest, an appropriate site needs to be selected. Each species has its own nest-building routine, which is strictly followed. In some species—Wilson's Warbler, for example—the female chooses the site and constructs the nest with the male offering only an occasional suggestion.

Nesting material usually consists of natural elements found in the immediate area. Most nests consist of plant fibers (such as bark peeled from grapevines), sticks, mud, dried grass, feathers, fur, or soft fuzzy tufts from thistle. Some birds, including Rufous Hummingbirds, use spider webs to glue nest materials together. Nesting material is limited to what a bird can hold or carry. Because of this, a bird must make many trips afield to gather enough materials to complete its nest. Most nests take at least four days or more, and hundreds, if not thousands, of trips to build.

As you'll see in the following illustrations, birds build a wide variety of nest types.

ground nest   **platform nest**   **cup nest**   **pendulous nest**

The simple **ground nest** is scraped out of the earth. A shallow depression that usually contains no nesting material, it is made by birds such as the Killdeer and Horned Lark.

Another kind of nest, the **platform nest**, represents a more complex type of nest building. Constructed of small twigs and branches, the platform nest is a simple arrangement of sticks which forms a platform and features a small depression to nestle the eggs.

Some platform nests, such as those of the Canada Goose, are constructed on the ground and are made with mud and grass. Platform nests can also be on cliffs, bridges, balconies or even in flowerpots. This kind of nest gives space to adventurous youngsters and functions as a landing platform for the parents. Many waterfowl construct platform nests on the ground, usually near water or actually in water. Floating platform nests vary with the water level, thus preventing nests with eggs from being flooded.

The **cup nest** is a modified platform nest, used by three-quarters of all songbirds. Constructed from the outside in, a supporting platform is constructed first. This platform is attached firmly to a tree, shrub, rock ledge or the ground. Next, the sides are constructed of grasses, small twigs, bark or leaves, which are woven together and often glued with mud for additional strength. The inner cup, lined with feathers, animal fur, soft plant material or animal hair, is constructed last. The mother bird uses her chest to cast the final contours of the inner nest.

The **pendulous nest** is an unusual nest, looking more like a sock hanging from a branch than a nest. Inaccessible to most predators, these nests are attached to the ends of the smallest branches of a tree, and often wave wildly in the breeze. Woven very tightly of plant fibers, they are strong and watertight, taking up to a week to build. More commonly used by tropical birds, this complicated nest type has also been mastered by kinglets. A small opening at the top or on the side of the nest allows parents access to the grass-lined interior. (It must be one heck of a ride to be inside one of these nests during a windy spring thunderstorm!)

Another type of nest, the **cavity nest**, is used by many birds, including woodpeckers and Mountain Bluebirds. The cavity nest is usually excavated in a tree branch or trunk and offers shelter from storms, sun, cold, wind and predators. A relatively small entrance hole in a tree leads to an inner chamber up to 10 inches (25 cm) below. Usually constructed by woodpeckers, the cavity nest is typically used only once by its builder, but subsequently can be used for many years by birds such as Tree Swallows, mergansers and bluebirds, which do not have the capability of excavating one for themselves. Kingfishers, on the other hand, excavate a tunnel up to 4 feet (1 m) long, which connects the entrance in a riverbank to the nest chamber. These cavity nests are often sparsely lined because they are already well insulated.

Some birds, including some swallows, take nest building one step further. They use a collection of small balls of mud to construct an adobe-style home. Constructed beneath the eaves of houses, under bridges or inside chimneys, some of these nests look like simple cup nests. Others are completely enclosed, with small tunnel-like openings that lead into a safe nesting chamber for the baby birds.

Who Builds the Nest?

In general, the female bird builds the nest. She gathers nesting materials and constructs a nest, with an occasional visit from her mate to check on the progress. In some species, both parents contribute equally to the construction of a nest. A male bird might forage for precisely the right sticks, grass or mud, but it's often the female that forms or puts together the nest. She uses her body to form the egg chamber. Rarely does the male build a nest by himself.

Fledging

Fledging is the interval between hatching and flight or leaving the nest. Some birds leave the nest within hours of hatching (precocial), but it might be weeks before they are able to fly. This is common with waterfowl and shorebirds. Until they start to fly, they are called fledglings. Birds that are still in the nest are called nestlings. Other baby birds are born naked and blind, and remain in the nest for several weeks (altricial).

Why Birds Migrate

Why do birds migrate? The short answer is simple–food. Birds migrate to areas with high concentrations of food, as it is easier to breed where food is than where it is not. A typical migrating bird–the Orange-crowned Warbler, for instance–will migrate from the tropics of Central and South America to nest in the forests of Alaska, taking advantage of billions of newly hatched insects to feed its young. This trip is called **complete migration**.

Some birds of prey return from their complete migration to northern regions that are overflowing with small rodents such as mice and voles that have continued to breed in winter.

Complete migrators have a set time and pattern of migration. Each year at nearly the same time, they take off and head for a specific wintering ground. Complete migrators may travel great distances, sometimes as much as 15,000 miles (24,150 km) or more in a year. But complete migration doesn't necessarily imply flying to and from a tropical destination. The Dark-eyed Junco, for example, is a complete migrator that flies back from the lower 48 states and Canada to spend the summer right here in Alaska. This is still called complete migration.

There are many interesting aspects to complete migrators. In the spring, males usually migrate several weeks before the females, arriving early to scope out possibilities for nesting sites and food sources, and to begin to defend territories. The females arrive several weeks later. In the autumn, in many species, the females and their young leave early, often up to four weeks before the adult males.

All migrators are not the same type. **Partial migrators** such as Red-necked Grebes usually wait until the food supply dwindles before moving to the coast. Unlike complete migrators, partial migrators move only far enough south, or sometimes east and west, to find abundant food. In some years it might be only a few hundred miles. In other years it might be nearly a thousand. This kind of migration, dependent on weather and availability of food, is sometimes called seasonal movement.

Unlike the predictable ebbing and flowing behavior of complete migrators or partial migrators, **irruptive migrators** can move every third to fifth year or, in some cases, in consecutive years. These migrations are triggered when times are really tough and food is scarce. The Common Redpoll is a good example of an irruptive migrator, because it leaves its normal northern range in search of food or in response to overpopulation.

How Do Birds Migrate?

One of the many secrets of migration is fat. While we humans are fighting the battle of the bulge, birds intentionally gorge themselves to put on as much fat as possible while still being able to fly. Fat provides the greatest amount of energy per unit of weight, and in the same way that your car needs gas, birds are propelled by fat and stalled without it.

During long migratory flights, fat deposits are used up quickly, and birds need to stop to "refuel." This is when backyard bird feeding stations and undeveloped, natural spaces around our towns and cities are especially important. Some birds require up to 2-3 days of constant feeding to build their fat reserves before continuing their seasonal trip.

Some birds such as most eagles, hawks, ospreys and falcons migrate during the day. Larger birds can hold more body fat, go longer without eating and take longer to migrate. These birds glide along on rising columns of warm air, called thermals, which hold them aloft while they slowly make their way north or south. They generally rest at night and hunt early in the morning before the sun has a chance to warm up the land and create good soaring conditions. Birds migrating during the day use a combination of landforms, rivers, and the rising and setting sun to guide them in the right direction.

Most other birds migrate during the night. Studies show that some birds which migrate at night use the stars to navigate. Others use the setting sun, while still others such as doves use the earth's magnetic fields to guide them north or south. While flying at night might seem like a crazy idea, nocturnal migration is safer for several reasons. First, there are fewer nighttime predators for migrating birds. Second, traveling at night allows time during the day to find food in unfamiliar surroundings. Finally, nighttime wind patterns tend to be flat, or laminar. These flat winds don't have the turbulence associated with daytime winds and can actually help carry smaller birds by pushing them along.

HOW TO USE THIS GUIDE

To help you quickly and easily identify birds, this book is organized by color. Simply note the color of the bird and turn to that section. Refer to the first page for the color key. The male Downy Woodpecker, for example, is black and white with a red mark on its head. Because the bird is mostly black and white, it will be found in the black and white section. Each color section is also arranged by size, generally with the smaller birds first. Sections may also incorporate the average size in a range, which, in some cases, reflects size differences between the male and female birds. Flip through the pages in that color section to find the bird. If you already know the name of the bird, check the index for the page number. In some species, the male and female are remarkably different in color. In others, the color of the breeding and winter plumages differs. These species have an inset photograph with a page reference and, in most cases, are found in two color sections.

In the description section you will find a variety of information about the bird. On page 1 is a sample of the information that is included in the book.

Range Maps

Range maps are included for each bird. Colored areas indicate where in Alaska a particular bird is most likely to be found. The colors represent the presence of a species during a specific season, not the density or amount of birds in the area. Green is used for summer, blue for winter, red for year-round and yellow for areas where the bird is seen during migration. While every effort has been made to accurately depict these ranges, they are only general guidelines. Ranges actually change on an ongoing basis due to a variety of factors. Changes in the weather, species abundance, landscape and vital resources such as the availability of food and water can affect local populations, migration and movements, causing birds to be found in areas that are atypical for the species.

Colored areas simply mean bird sightings for that species have been frequent in those areas and less frequent in the others. Please use the maps as intended–as general guides only.

YEAR-ROUND
MIGRATION
SUMMER
WINTER

Common Name

Range Map   *Scientific name*   Color Indicator

Size: measures head to tail, may include wingspan

Male: a brief description of the male bird, and may include breeding, winter or other plumages

Female: a brief description of the female bird, which is sometimes not the same as the male

Juvenile: a brief description of the juvenile bird, which often looks like the female

Nest: the kind of nest this bird builds to raise its young; who builds the nest; how many broods per year

Eggs: how many eggs you might expect to see in a nest; color and marking

Incubation: the average time parents spend incubating the eggs; who does the incubation

Fledging: the average time young spend in the nest after hatching but before they leave the nest; who does the most "childcare" and feeding

Migration: complete (consistent, seasonal), partial (seasonal movement, destination varies), irruptive (unpredictable, depends on the food supply), non-migrator; additional comments

Food: what the bird eats most of the time (e.g., seeds, insects, fruit, nectar, small mammals, fish); if it typically comes to a bird feeding station

Compare: notes about other birds that look similar and the pages on which they can be found, may include extra information to help identify

Stan's Notes: Interesting gee-whiz natural history information. This could be something to look or listen for, or something to help positively identify the bird. Also includes remarkable features.

1

winter

breeding

European Starling
Sturnus vulgaris

YEAR-ROUND
SUMMER

Size: 7½" (19 cm)

Male: Gray-to-black bird with white speckles in autumn and winter. Shiny purple black in spring and summer. Bill color changes with the seasons from yellow in spring to gray in autumn. Short tail.

Female: same as male

Juvenile: similar to adult, gray brown in color with a streaked chest

Nest: cavity; male and female line cavity; 2 broods per year

Eggs: 4-6; bluish with brown markings

Incubation: 12-14 days; female and male incubate

Fledging: 18-20 days; female and male feed young

Migration: partial to non-migrator; will move around to find food

Food: insects, seeds, fruit; comes to seed and suet feeders

Compare: An urban bird that is not confused with other birds. Look for a long pointed bill and stubby tail to help identify. Usually seen in small to large flocks.

Stan's Notes: A great songster, this bird can mimic other birds and sounds. Often displaces woodpeckers, chickadees and other cavity-nesting birds. Can be very aggressive and destroy eggs or young of other birds. Bill changes color with the seasons: yellow in spring and gray in autumn. Gathers in the hundreds in autumn. Not a native bird, it was introduced to New York City in 1890-91 from Europe.

3

female pg. 137

male

SUMMER

Red-winged Blackbird
Agelaius phoeniceus

Size: 8½" (22 cm)

Male: Jet black bird with red and yellow shoulder patches on upper wings. Pointed black bill.

Female: heavily streaked brown bird with a pointed brown bill and white eyebrows

Juvenile: same as female

Nest: cup; female builds; 2-3 broods per year

Eggs: 3-4; bluish green with brown markings

Incubation: 10-12 days; female incubates

Fledging: 11-14 days; female and male feed young

Migration: complete, to western states

Food: seeds, insects; will come to seed feeders

Compare: Slightly smaller than male Rusty Blackbird (pg. 7). Differs from all other blackbirds due to the red and yellow patches on its wings (epaulets).

Stan's Notes: Summer resident in southeastern Alaska. It is a sure sign of spring when Red-winged Blackbirds return to the marshes. Flocks of up to 100,000 birds have been reported. Males return to Alaska before females and defend their territories by singing from the tops of surrounding vegetation. Males repeat their call from the tops of cattails while showing off their red and yellow wing bars (epaulets). Females choose a mate and will often nest over shallow water in thick stands of cattails. Red-wingeds feed mostly on seeds in fall and spring, switching to insects during summer.

female pg. 261

male

SUMMER

Rusty Blackbird
Euphagus carolinus

Size: 9" (22.5 cm)

Male: Glossy black blackbird with blue and purple highlights. Bright yellow eyes. A short, thin pointed bill. Non-breeding plumage is more rusty brown than glossy black.

Female: overall gray blackbird with rusty edges of feathers, yellow eyes, a short, thin pointed bill, non-breeding is much browner with a gray rump and black patch around each eye

Juvenile: similar to female

Nest: cup; female builds; 1-2 broods per year

Eggs: 4-5; bluish with brown markings

Incubation: 12-14 days; female incubates

Fledging: 11-13 days; male and female feed young

Migration: complete, to eastern states

Food: insects, seeds

Compare: The male Red-winged Blackbird (pg. 5) has red and yellow markings on its shoulders and is slightly smaller in size.

Stan's Notes: This bird nests across most of Alaska in small loose colonies, often preferring more wooded, swampy areas. Male feeds female while she incubates. Gathers in large groups. Flocks with other blackbirds to migrate in autumn. When in flight, the end of tail often appears squared.

Northwestern Crow
Corvus caurinus

YEAR-ROUND

Size: 16" (40 cm)

Male: Completely black with a black bill, legs and feet. Can have a purple sheen in direct sun.

Female: same as male

Juvenile: similar to adult

Nest: platform; female builds; 1 brood per year

Eggs: 4-5; pale blue with brown markings

Incubation: 16-20 days; female incubates

Fledging: 28-35 days; female and male feed young

Migration: non-migrator; will move around in winter to find food

Food: insects, fruit, seeds, fish, small mammals, carrion; comes to seed and ground feeders

Compare: The Northwestern Crow is smaller than the Common Raven (pg. 17), but lacks shaggy throat feathers and has a smaller bill and a lower pitched, more hoarse call.

Stan's Notes: One of the most recognizable birds in Alaska. Often reuses nest every year if not taken over by a hawk or owl. Collects and stores bright, shiny objects in nest. Can mimic other birds and human voices. One of the smartest birds and very social. Entertains itself by provoking chases with other birds and animals. Feeds on road kill, but is rarely hit by cars. Cooperative hunting, with one crow sitting in a tree to watch for traffic while the other walks out to feed on the carrion. Extended families roost together at night in winter and communicate the location of food. In the morning the group flies to the food source. Unmated birds from the previous year help parents raise the current year's young. Can live 20 years.

YEAR-ROUND
SUMMER

Black Oystercatcher
Haematopus bachmani

Size: 18" (45 cm)

Male: An overall black body with a bright reddish orange, heavy straight bill. Yellow eyes with a red outline. Yellow legs and feet. Stocky body with a short tail and broad wings, as seen in flight.

Female: same as male

Juvenile: similar to adult, with light brown body and dull orange, black-tipped bill

Nest: ground; female and male construct; 1 brood per year

Eggs: 1-3; dull white to olive with brown marks

Incubation: 24-29 days, female incubates

Fledging: 35-40 days; female and male feed young

Migration: non-migrator to partial in Alaska

Food: insects, mollusks, worms, crustaceans

Compare: The breeding Black-bellied Plover (pg. 43) has white on its head and a black and white back. Black Turnstone (pg. 35) lacks yellow eyes outlined in red. Look for the stocky body and red-orange bill of Oystercatcher.

Stan's Notes: A shorebird found mainly along rocky shores. Rarely seen away from coast. Often alone and not approachable. Common name comes from its ability to feed on oysters and mussels. Uses its large bill to pry or sometimes chisel shells open with hammer-like blows. Believed to have a long-term pair bond. A noisy courtship display with much mutual bowing. Nest is a scrape on the ground, sometimes lined with shells and rocks, built above the high tide.

female pg. 197

male

Black Scoter
Melanitta nigra

MIGRATION
SUMMER
WINTER

Size: 19¼" (49 cm)

Male: All-black duck with a large yellow knob at the base of bill and a narrow pointed tail.

Female: brown duck with a dark crown, pale white cheeks and thin dark bill

Juvenile: similar to female

Nest: ground; female builds; 1 brood per year

Eggs: 6-8; light pink to buff without markings

Incubation: 30-31 days; female incubates

Fledging: 45-50 days; female feeds young

Migration: complete, to southern coastal Alaska, western coastal U.S. and Mexico

Food: mollusks, crustaceans, aquatic plants, seeds

Compare: Smaller than the male White-winged Scoter (pg. 15), which has a white comma-shaped patch beneath each eye and a yellow and orange bill. Slightly smaller than male Surf Scoter (pg. 69), which has a white patch on forehead and nape and a multicolored bill.

Stan's Notes: The least common of scoters, although once known as the Common Scoter. Often in mixed flocks numbering in the hundreds along the coast during migration and winter. Usually will feed in seawater 20-40 feet (6-12 m) deep, just outside the breaker zone. Nests on the tundra close to freshwater lakes and ponds, returning to sea after breeding season for the rest of the summer and winter. Female doesn't breed until her third summer. Male will leave female shortly after she starts to incubate. Broods sometimes gather in groups called crèches and are tended by 1-3 older females.

female pg. 201

male

MIGRATION
SUMMER
WINTER

White-winged Scoter
Melanitta fusca

Size: 20½" (52 cm)

Male: A black duck with a white comma-shaped patch underneath each eye. Large bicolored yellow and orange bill. Bright white eyes.

Female: brown duck with a dark crown, large dull white patch just behind the eyes and at the base of a large dark bill

Juvenile: similar to female

Nest: ground; female builds; 1 brood per year

Eggs: 5-10; light pink to buff without markings

Incubation: 28-31 days; female incubates

Fledging: 50-60 days; female feeds young

Migration: complete, to southern coastal Alaska, western coastal U.S. and Mexico

Food: mollusks, crustaceans, aquatic insects and plants

Compare: Larger than the male Black Scoter (pg. 13), which lacks the white mark beneath each eye. Slightly larger than male Surf Scoter (pg. 69), which has a multicolored bill and white patch on the forehead and nape.

Stan's Notes: Nests on the tundra in Alaska near freshwater lakes and ponds. Spends the winter at sea, rarely returning to shore. Sometimes in mixed flocks with other scoters. The genus name *Melanitta* from the Greek *melas* for "black" and *netta* for "duck" describes the bird well. The common name was first used in the *Collective Catalogue of Birds* (1674), but its origins are unknown.

in flight

YEAR-ROUND

Common Raven
Corvus corax

Size: 22-27" (56-69 cm)

Male: Large all-black bird with a large black bill, a shaggy beard of feathers on the chin and throat, and a large wedge-shaped tail, seen in flight.

Female: same as male

Juvenile: same as adult

Nest: platform; female and male build; 1 brood per year

Eggs: 4-6; pale green with brown markings

Incubation: 18-21 days; female incubates

Fledging: 38-44 days; female and male feed young

Migration: non-migrator; moves around to find food

Food: insects, fruit, small animals, carrion

Compare: Northwestern Crow (pg. 9) is smaller, lacks shaggy throat feathers and has a smaller bill and a lower pitched, more hoarse call. The Common Raven glides on flat outstretched wings unlike the constant flapping of the Northwestern Crow.

Stan's Notes: Considered by some to be the smartest of all birds. Known for its aerial acrobatics and long swooping dives. Sometimes scavenges with crows and gulls. Known to follow wolf packs around to pick up scraps and pick at bones of a kill. A cooperative hunter, often communicating the location of a good food source to other ravens. Complex courtship includes grabbing bills, preening each other and cooing. Most begin to breed at 3-4 years. Mates for life. Uses same nest site for many years.

drying

YEAR-ROUND
SUMMER

Pelagic Cormorant
Phalacrocorax pelagicus

Size: 28" (71 cm)

Male: A large black water bird that appears glossy green in direct sun. Long, snake-like white-washed neck. A long dark bill with a small orange patch at the base.

Female: same as male

Juvenile: similar to adult

Nest: platform, on a cliff in a colony; male and female build; 1 brood per year

Eggs: 3-5; light blue without markings

Incubation: 26-31 days; female and male incubate

Fledging: 37-45 days; female and male feed young

Migration: non-migrator to partial, to southern coastal Alaska

Food: small fish, aquatic insects

Compare: Smaller than the Double-crested Cormorant (pg. 21), which has a larger gray bill with yellow at the base and a hooked tip.

Stan's Notes: Found exclusively around rocky ocean shores. Often seen flying low over the water's surface, moving from one rocky outcropping to another. Excellent vision in the air and underwater. Feeds mainly on fish, diving to depths over 100 feet (30 m). Nests on steep, rocky inaccessible cliffs for protection from predators. One mate will gather nesting material such as small sticks, seaweed and other debris, and the other builds. Uses the same nest each year, adding new material each season. Older nests can reach 5-6 feet (1.5-1.8 m) tall. Young hatch several days apart (asynchronously).

in flight

juvenile

drying

Double-crested Cormorant
Phalacrocorax auritus

Size: 33" (84 cm)

Male: A large black water bird with a long snake-like neck. Long gray bill with yellow at the base and a hooked tip.

Female: same as male

Juvenile: lighter brown with a grayish chest and neck

Nest: platform, in colony; male and female build; 1 brood per year

Eggs: 3-4; bluish white without markings

Incubation: 25-29 days; female and male incubate

Fledging: 37-42 days; male and female feed young

Migration: non-migrator

Food: small fish, aquatic insects

Compare: Pelagic Cormorant (pg. 19) is smaller, has a smaller bill and lacks the yellow patch at base of bill and the hooked tip.

Stan's Notes: Often seen flying in large V formation. Usually roosts in large groups in trees close to water. Catches fish by swimming underwater with wings held at its sides. Lacks the oil gland that keeps feathers from becoming waterlogged. To dry off it strikes an erect pose with wings outstretched, facing the sun. Common name refers to its nearly invisible crests. "Cormorant" comes from the Latin *corvus*, meaning "crow," and *L. marinus*, meaning "pertaining to the sea," literally, "Sea Crow."

male

female

SUMMER

Blackpoll Warbler
Dendroica striata

Size: 5½" (14 cm)

Male: Overall black and white with a distinctive black cap. White face below the eyes. Fine, vertical dark streaking on breast and flanks. Short dark bill. Short tail with white undertail. Yellow legs and feet.

Female: pale black and white, appearing gray with faint streaks on the breast and flanks, white undertail, yellow legs, lacks a black cap

Juvenile: similar to female, with a wash of pale yellow and a gray nape of neck

Nest: cup; female builds; 1 brood per year

Eggs: 3-5; white with brown markings

Incubation: 12-14 days; female incubates

Fledging: 11-12 days; female and male feed young

Migration: complete, to South America

Food: insects, seeds, berries

Compare: Northern Waterthrush (pg. 113) and Arctic Warbler (pg. 231) have a light stripe above eyes and lack the male Blackpoll's black cap.

Stan's Notes: A relatively large-bodied warbler that nests in spruce woods in Alaska. Builds nest near the trunk of a tree, where there is support from a horizontal branch. Usually a bulky nest of twigs, bark and grasses with a feather lining. A true migrant, making a roundtrip of at least 2,500 miles (4,025 km) to South America. Females return to the nesting area the following year and mate with the male in the nearest territory. Males molt in late summer and appear like females during autumn migration.

male

winter male

female

YEAR-ROUND
MIGRATION
SUMMER
WINTER

Snow Bunting
Plectrophenax nivalis

Size: 6½" (16 cm)

Male: Winter plumage bunting has a white chin, breast and belly. Rusty brown head, back and shoulders. Small yellow bill. Black legs and feet. Breeding plumage is overall white with black and white wings.

Female: similar to breeding male, but lacks the all-white head

Juvenile: similar to winter male

Nest: cavity; female builds; 1-2 broods per year

Eggs: 4-7; green to blue with brown markings

Incubation: 10-16 days; female incubates

Fledging: 10-17 days; male and female feed young

Migration: complete to non-migrator in Alaska

Food: insects, seeds

Compare: This bird is easy to identify since no other small sparrow-like bird has so much white.

Stan's Notes: Seen throughout Alaska. Often feeds on the ground along roads. Usually seen in flocks of up to 30 individuals of mixed ages and sexes. Individual Snow Buntings appear slightly different from each other; some are completely black and white, others are a combination of black, white, brown and rust. Winter plumage is seen from September to March. Sometimes seen with summer birds such as Horned Larks and Lapland Longspurs. Female constructs a grass and moss nest in a cavity or on a cliff that is well protected from the weather. Young hatch at different times, so some leave the nest before others.

male

female

YEAR-ROUND

Downy Woodpecker
Picoides pubescens

Size: 6½" (16 cm)

Male: A small woodpecker with an all-white belly, black-and-white spotted wings, a black line running through the eyes, a short black bill, a white stripe down the back and red mark on the back of the head. Several small black spots along the sides of white tail.

Female: same as male, but lacks a red mark on head

Juvenile: same as female, some have a red mark near the forehead

Nest: cavity; male and female excavate; 1 brood per year

Eggs: 3-5; white without markings

Incubation: 11-12 days; female and male incubate, the female incubates during day, male at night

Fledging: 20-25 days; male and female feed young

Migration: non-migrator

Food: insects, seeds, visits seed and suet feeders

Compare: Almost identical to the Hairy Woodpecker (pg. 31), but smaller. Look for the shorter, thinner bill of Downy to differentiate them.

Stan's Notes: A year-round resident in parts of Alaska where trees are present. Stiff tail feathers help brace it like a tripod as it clings to a tree. Like all woodpeckers, it has a long barbed tongue to pull bugs from tiny places. Both sexes drum on branches or hollow logs to announce territories, which are rarely larger than 5 acres (2 ha). Male performs most brooding. Will winter roost in cavity. Doesn't breed in high elevations, but often moves there in winter for food.

male

female

YEAR-ROUND

American Three-toed Woodpecker
Picoides dorsalis

Size: 8½" (22 cm)

Male: Mostly black with a white chin, breast and belly. Heavy black barring on the flanks and irregular white barring on back. Black line from base of bill to cheek. Yellow cap.

Female: similar to male, lacks a yellow cap

Juvenile: similar to male, often a larger yellow cap

Nest: cavity; male and female excavate; 1 brood per year

Eggs: 2-6; white without markings

Incubation: 12-14 days; female and male incubate, the female incubates during day, male at night

Fledging: 22-26 days; female and male feed young

Migration: non-migrator

Food: insects

Compare: The Black-backed Woodpecker (pg. 31) is larger, with a well-defined yellow cap and a solid black back. Male Hairy Woodpecker (pg. 33) is slightly larger and has a white stripe down the back and red mark on the back of head.

Stan's Notes: Was at one time considered the same species as the Black-backed Woodpecker. Most other woodpeckers have four toes on each foot, two forward and two rear. Lacks an inner rear-facing toe, resulting in three toes on each foot, hence its common name. Mated pairs may remain together year-round and mate for several consecutive years. Mates forage for food separately, usually low in trees. Nests in loose colonies, often near an abundant food source.

male

female

YEAR-ROUND

Hairy Woodpecker

Picoides villosus

Size: 9" (22.5 cm)

Male: Black-and-white woodpecker with a white belly, and black wings with rows of white spots. White stripe down back. Long black bill. Red mark on back of head.

Female: same as male, but lacks a red mark on head

Juvenile: grayer version of female

Nest: cavity; female and male excavate; 1 brood per year

Eggs: 3-6, white without markings

Incubation: 11-15 days; female and male incubate, the female incubates during day, male at night

Fledging: 28-30 days; male and female feed young

Migration: non-migrator

Food: insects, nuts, seeds; comes to seed and suet feeders

Compare: Larger than Downy Woodpecker (pg. 27) and has a longer, thicker bill that is nearly as long as the width of its head.

Stan's Notes: Found year-round in wooded areas in southeastern Alaska. Before landing on bird feeders, announces its arrival with a sharp chirp. Responsible for eating many destructive forest insects. Has a barbed tongue, which helps it extract insects from trees. Tiny bristle-like feathers at the base of bill protect its nostrils from wood dust. Drums on hollow logs, branches or stovepipes in springtime to announce its territory. Often prefers to excavate nest cavities in live aspen trees. Has a larger, more oval-shaped cavity entrance than that of the Downy Woodpecker.

male

female

YEAR-ROUND

Black-backed Woodpecker
Picoides arcticus

Size: 9½" (24 cm)

Male: Mostly black with a white chin, breast and belly. Heavy black barring on flanks. Black line from base of bill to cheek. Yellow cap.

Female: similar to male, lacks a yellow cap

Juvenile: similar to male, often a larger yellow cap

Nest: cavity; male and female excavate; 1 brood per year

Eggs: 2-6; white without markings

Incubation: 12-14 days; female and male incubate

Fledging: 21-25 days; female and male feed young

Migration: non-migrator

Food: insects

Compare: The American Three-toed Woodpecker (pg. 29) has white barring on the back and a less defined yellow cap. The male Hairy Woodpecker (pg. 31) is slightly smaller and has a white stripe down the back and a red mark on back of head.

Stan's Notes: Lacking an inner rear-facing toe, this bird is a close relative of the American Three-toed Woodpecker. Usually seen in recently dead trees from insect damage or fire. Named for its black back. Its white breast often becomes dark and sooty when feeding in a fire-damaged forest, making it appear all black. Feeds mainly on larvae of wood-boring beetles. Some estimate one woodpecker can eat more than 13,000 larvae annually. Species name *arcticus* is Greek for "near the bear" and refers to the Great Bear constellation in the northern sky and its northern range.

MIGRATION
SUMMER

Black Turnstone
Arenaria melanocephala

Size: 9½" (24 cm)

Male: Breeding (Apr-Aug) is overall black to dark gray with a white belly and white mark at base of bill. Short dark bill. Dark legs. Non-breeding (Aug-Apr) lacks the white mark at base of bill.

Female: same as male

Juvenile: similar to non-breeding adult, more gray

Nest: ground; male and female construct; 1 brood per year

Eggs: 3-4; yellow with brown markings

Incubation: 21-22 days; male and female incubate

Fledging: 18-20 days; female and male feed young

Migration: complete, to western coastal U.S., Mexico

Food: aquatic insects, barnacles, mollusks, snails

Compare: Ruddy Turnstone (pg. 37) has black and chestnut wings and a black and white head. Black Oystercatcher (pg. 11) has yellow eyes outlined in red and a large red-orange bill.

Stan's Notes: Closely related to the Ruddy Turnstone. Seen mainly on rocky shores and beaches and, to a lesser degree, mud flats. The common name "Turnstone" comes from the habit of using its short, thick, slightly upturned bill to flip or turn over stones in search of food. Walks along rocky shores in a toylike fashion, seeming to be always on the move. Males will perform an aerial display during courtship. Nest is only a slight depression on the ground lined with dead grasses or mud, usually located close to water. Semi-colony nester, with both parents incubating eggs and brooding the young.

non-breeding

breeding

Ruddy Turnstone
Arenaria interpres

Size: 9½" (24 cm)

Male: Breeding has orange legs, a black and white head marking, black bib, white breast and belly, black and chestnut wings and back. Slightly upturned black bill. Non-breeding has a brown and white head and breast.

Female: similar to male, only duller

Juvenile: similar to adults, but black and white head has a scaly appearance

Nest: ground; female builds; 1 brood per year

Eggs: 3-4; olive green with dark markings

Incubation: 22-24 days; male and female incubate

Fledging: 19-21 days; male feeds young

Migration: complete, to coastal California and Mexico

Food: aquatic insects, fish, mollusks, crustaceans, worms, eggs

Compare: Black Turnstone (pg. 35) is overall black with dark legs. Look for orange legs and a bold pattern on head and neck to identify.

Stan's Notes: Summer resident and migrant in Alaska. Also called Rock Plover. Was named "Turnstone" because it turns stones over on rocky beaches to find food. Known for its unusual behavior of robbing and eating other birds' eggs. Will hang around crabbing operations to eat scraps from nets. Can be very tolerant of humans when feeding. Females usually leave before their young leave the nests (fledge), resulting in males raising the young. Males have a bare spot on the belly (brood patch) to warm the young, something only females normally have.

YEAR-ROUND

Ancient Murrelet
Synthliboramphus antiquus

Size: 10" (25 cm)

Male: A small black and white bird with a very short, thick neck and tiny yellow-tipped bill. Black head and throat. Bright white on the neck. Distinctive white eyebrows.

Female: same as male

Juvenile: similar to adult, lacks white eyebrows and a black throat

Nest: cavity; male and female excavate; 1 brood per year

Eggs: 1-2; tan with brown markings

Incubation: 33-36 days; female and male incubate

Fledging: 35-40 days; male and female feed young

Migration: non-migrator; remains at sea except to nest

Food: aquatic insects, small fish

Compare: Smaller than the Common Murre (pg. 57) which has a much larger, longer bill. Look for the white eyebrows to help identify.

Stan's Notes: Spends its time at sea (pelagic), coming to land only to nest each spring. Nests in large colonies in burrows under rocks and logs or in natural underground cavities. Breeding pair will dig a burrow down to 4 feet (1 m). Adults may mate for life, returning to the same nest burrow for many years. One parent will go out to sea to search for food, causing the other to incubate for up to 3 days nonstop before the mate returns. Parents switch incubating at night. Young leave the nest burrow at 2-3 days of age and move out to sea, using the cover of night to avoid predators such as gulls and falcons.

breeding
male

breeding
female

non-breeding
pg. 275

MIGRATION
SUMMER

American Golden-Plover
Pluvialis dominica

Size: 11" (28 cm)

Male: Breeding (Apr-Sep) has a striking black face, neck, belly and undertail. Dark cap. White forehead with white extending to eyebrows and down the sides of neck. Dark back with golden highlights. Long dark legs and short black bill. Gray wing linings, seen in flight.

Female: similar to breeding male

Juvenile: similar to non-breeding adult

Nest: ground; male builds; 1 brood per year

Eggs: 3-4; cream with brown markings

Incubation: 26-28 days; male and female incubate

Fledging: 20-22 days; male and female show young what to eat

Migration: complete, to South America

Food: insects, fruit, seeds

Compare: Similar size as breeding Black-bellied Plover (pg. 43), which has a white undertail and rump. Look for the breeding American Golden-Plover's black undertail and dark cap to help identify. When it is in flight, also look for gray wing linings to help identify.

Stan's Notes: This bird was formerly called Lesser Golden-Plover. Was once hunted by market hunters. More than 48,000 birds were reported to have been shot in one day near New Orleans in 1861. Populations were extremely depleted by the early 1900s. May mate for life. Male does most of the nest selection and construction. Male also incubates most of the time. Both sexes feed the young equally.

non-breeding
pg. 277

breeding

Black-bellied Plover
Pluvialis squatarola

Size: 11-12" (28-30 cm)

Male: Striking black and white breeding plumage. A black belly, breast, sides, face and neck. White cap, nape of neck and belly near tail. Black legs and bill.

Female: less black on belly and breast than male

Juvenile: grayer than adults, with much less black

Nest: ground; male and female construct; 1 brood per year

Eggs: 3-4; pinkish or greenish with black brown markings

Incubation: 26-27 days; male and female incubate, male incubates during the day, female at night

Fledging: 35-45 days; male feeds young, young learn quickly to feed themselves

Migration: complete, to coastal California and Mexico

Food: insects

Compare: The breeding Dunlin (pg. 139) is slightly smaller, with a rusty back and long down-curved bill. Look for a large black patch on the belly, face and breast and a white cap.

Stan's Notes: Male performs a "butterfly" courtship flight to attract females. Female leaves the male and young about 12 days after the eggs hatch. Starts breeding at 3 years of age. Migrant and summer resident along coastal Alaska. In flight, in any plumage, it displays a white rump and stripe on wings with black axillaries (armpits). Often darts across the ground to grab an insect and run.

female pg. 161

male

Bufflehead
Bucephala albeola

MIGRATION
SUMMER
WINTER

Size: 13-15" (33-38 cm)

Male: A small duck with striking white sides and black back. Green purple head with a large white bonnet-like patch.

Female: brown version of male, with a brown head and white patch on cheek, just behind eyes

Juvenile: similar to female

Nest: cavity; female lines old woodpecker cavity; 1 brood per year

Eggs: 8-10; ivory to olive without markings

Incubation: 29-31 days; female incubates

Fledging: 50-55 days; female leads young to food

Migration: complete, to southern coastal Alaska, western states, Mexico and Central America

Food: aquatic insects

Compare: A small black and white diving duck. Look for the green purple head with a large white patch to help identify the male Bufflehead.

Stan's Notes: Common diving duck that travels with other ducks. Found on rivers and lakes. Nests in old woodpecker cavities. Has been known to use a burrow in an earthen bank when tree cavities are scarce. Will use a nest box. Uses only down feathers to line the nest cavity. Unlike other ducks, young remain in the nest for up to two days before venturing out with their mother. Female is very territorial and remains with the same mate for many years.

YEAR-ROUND
SUMMER

Horned Puffin
Fratercula corniculata

Size: 15" (38 cm)

Male: Large white and black head. Black back and wings. Enormous yellow bill with an orange tip. White chest, belly and underside of tail. Winter lacks a bold white and black pattern on head and has a dark bill with orange tip.

Female: same as male

Juvenile: similar to winter adult

Nest: cavity; male and female excavate; 1 brood per year

Eggs: 1; bluish white with gray markings

Incubation: 40-41 days; male and female incubate

Fledging: 40-45 days; male and female feed young

Migration: partial to non-migrator, along the West coast from Alaska to Washington

Food: fish, aquatic insects, squid, mollusks, algae, urchins

Compare: Same size and similar shape as the Tufted Puffin (pg. 49), which has a black belly and an enormous orange bill.

Stan's Notes: Colony nester on rocky islands with steep cliffs. Digs a burrow under a turf-covered slope down to 4 feet (1 m), ending in a nest chamber. Often silent; may give a low rumbling, groaning sound in colony. Usually flies up to 30 feet (9 m) above the water's surface; most other sea birds will fly only 5-10 feet (1.5-3 m) above the surface. A slow flyer compared with other sea birds. Parents find food for their young, returning with many fish lined up in their bills. Parents locate offspring by their individual calls.

YEAR-ROUND
SUMMER

Tufted Puffin
Fratercula cirrhata

Size: 15" (38 cm)

Male: All-black body with a large white and black head and pale yellow feather tufts at back of head. An enormous orange bill. Winter lacks the bold white and black pattern on head and has a pale orange bill.

Female: same as male

Juvenile: similar to winter adult

Nest: cavity; male and female excavate; 1 brood per year

Eggs: 1; bluish white with gray markings

Incubation: 40-41 days; male and female incubate

Fledging: 40-45 days; male and female feed young

Migration: partial to non-migrator, along the West coast from Alaska to Washington

Food: fish, aquatic insects, squid, mollusks, algae, urchins

Compare: Same size and similar shape as the Horned Puffin (pg. 47), which has a white breast and belly and yellow at the base of bill.

Stan's Notes: Colony nester on rocky islands with steep cliffs. Digs a burrow under a turf-covered slope down to 8 feet (2 m), ending in a nesting chamber. Burrow is deeper than Horned Puffin's, but otherwise the biology is very similar. A silent bird when away from the colony. While in colony, it may give a low rumbling, groaning sound. Usually seen flying up to 30 feet (9 m) above the water's surface; most other sea birds will fly only 5-10 feet (1.5-3 m) above the surface. A slow flyer compared with other sea birds.

female pg. 171

male

SUMMER

Lesser Scaup
Aythya affinis

Size: 16-17" (40-43 cm)

Male: Appears mostly black with bold white sides and gray back. Chest and head look nearly black, but head appears purple with green highlights in direct sun. Bright yellow eyes.

Female: overall brown with dull white patch at base of light gray bill, yellow eyes

Juvenile: same as female

Nest: ground; female builds; 1 brood per year

Eggs: 8-14; olive buff without markings

Incubation: 22-28 days; female incubates

Fledging: 45-50 days; female teaches young to feed

Migration: complete, to western states and Mexico

Food: aquatic plants and insects

Compare: The male Greater Scaup (pg. 61) has a more rounded head. Male Common Goldeneye (pg. 67) has a white breast. The male Blue-winged Teal (pg. 165) has a white mark at base of bill. Male Canvasback (pg. 329) has a sloping forehead and long dark bill.

Stan's Notes: A common diving duck. Often seen in large flocks on lakes, ponds and sewage lagoons. Completely submerges itself to feed on the bottom of lakes (unlike dabbling ducks, which only tip forward to reach the bottom). Note the bold white stripe under the wings when in flight. Male leaves female when she starts to incubate the eggs. Quantity of eggs (clutch size) increases with the age of the female. An interesting baby-sitting arrangement in which groups of young (crèches) are tended by 1-3 adult females.

female pg. 173

male

Harlequin Duck

Histrionicus histrionicus

Size: 17" (43 cm)

Male: Breeding is black and white with rusty red sides and top of head. Highest part of head just above the eyes. Small light-colored bill. Long pointed tail. Winter is overall brown with a white patch at sides of head and at base of bill. Faint white marks at shoulders and base of tail.

Female: similar to winter male

Juvenile: similar to female

Nest: ground; female builds; 1 brood per year

Eggs: 6-8; pale white without markings

Incubation: 28-31 days; female incubates

Fledging: 60-70 days; female leads young to food

Migration: partial to non-migrator, to southern coastal Alaska

Food: aquatic insects, crustaceans, mollusks

Compare: The male Greater Scaup (pg. 61) and Lesser Scaup (pg. 51) are similar in size, but have white sides. Look for the unique black and white pattern and rust sides to help identify.

Stan's Notes: A small duck that rides low in water. Found in fast-running rivers and streams, which presumably have a richer food supply than slow-moving water. Frequently walks in shallow water, foraging for food on the bottom among the rocks. Uses wings and feet to propel itself underwater unlike other diving ducks, which just use their feet. Female does not breed until 2 years of age. Male leaves female after she starts to incubate.

in flight

male

winter male

female

Long-tailed Duck
Clangula hyemalis

MIGRATION
SUMMER
WINTER

Size: 17" (43 cm)

Male: Breeding (May-Oct) adult has a black head and neck and white face. Gray sides. Small dark bill with a tan ring. Very long, narrow tail. Winter (Nov-Apr) has a white neck and head with black and gray patches on face.

Female: overall brown with a dark face, white at the base of neck and around eyes, large white rump; winter has a white face and sides

Juvenile: similar to winter female

Nest: ground; female builds; 1 brood per year

Eggs: 6-8; pale green without markings

Incubation: 24-29 days; female incubates

Fledging: 35-40 days; female leads young to food

Migration: complete, to coastal Alaska and Canada

Food: aquatic insects

Compare: Breeding male Harlequin Duck (pg. 53) has rusty red sides and a shorter tail.

Stan's Notes: Southern coastal duck in winter. Moves across Alaska in spring and summer to breed. Adults molt up to four times per year. Some molt continuously, but the male's long tail is consistent and easily visible in flight. Fast flyers. Small groups fly just above the water's surface. One of the deepest diving ducks, diving down to 200 feet (60 m). Can stay submerged up to 1.5 minutes. Very vocal. The males have a yodeling call; females give soft calls and grunts. After hatching, young form groups (crèches) that usually consist of 3-4 broods (10-30 individuals), but may have up to 100 ducklings. Older females often tend crèches. Formerly called Oldsquaw.

YEAR-ROUND
SUMMER

Common Murre
Uria aalge

Size: 17½" (44 cm)

Male: Breeding (Mar-Sep) has a dark brown-to-black head, neck, back and sides. Lower half is white. A long, slender, pointed black bill. Winter (Sep-Mar) has a white throat, chin and cheeks, with a narrow black stripe arching from behind eyes to sides of neck.

Female: same as male

Juvenile: similar to winter adult

Nest: no nest; 1 brood per year

Eggs: 1; brown to olive (sometimes white) with brown markings

Incubation: 30-33 days; female and male incubate

Fledging: 19-25 days; male and female feed young

Migration: non-migrator to partial; moves away from northern Alaska in winter, farther out to sea

Food: small fish

Compare: Winter Thick-billed Murre (pg. 59) lacks a narrow black stripe behind the eyes. The Ancient Murrelet (pg. 39) has a tiny yellow-tipped bill and a very short, stout neck.

Stan's Notes: A colony nester on cliffs, with colonies numbering in the thousands. Pairs return to the same nest spot each year. Moves a few pebbles to build nest. High-density nesters, some so close they touch. Incubates in semi-upright position, holding the egg with its feet. Pairs may mate for life. Nearly wiped out by the mid-1800s due to unregulated hunting. Populations now stable. Highly susceptible to oil spills. Bald Eagles seem to prefer these birds in their diet.

breeding

winter

YEAR-ROUND
SUMMER
WINTER

Thick-billed Murre
Uria lomvia

Size: 18" (45 cm)

Male: Breeding (Mar-Sep) has a dark brown-to-black head, neck, back and sides. Lower half is white. A long, thick, pointed black bill, slightly down-curved at the tip. Winter (Sep-Mar) has a white throat and chin.

Female: same as male

Juvenile: similar to winter adult, but has a black and white speckled throat and chin

Nest: no nest; 1 brood per year

Eggs: 1; light blue to olive (sometimes white) with brown markings

Incubation: 30-35 days; female and male incubate

Fledging: 19-25 days; male and female feed young

Migration: non-migrator to partial; moves away from northern Alaska in winter, farther out to sea

Food: small fish

Compare: The winter Common Murre (pg. 57) has a narrow black stripe behind the eyes. The Ancient Murrelet (pg. 39) has a tiny yellow-tipped bill and a very short, stout neck.

Stan's Notes: Breeds on cliffs in very large colonies of over 10,000 pairs. Only 11 colonies compose nearly all of the breeding Thick-billed Murres. Adults mate for life, but are more likely committed to the nest site rather than to each other. Female incubates during the day, male mainly at night. Incubates egg by continuously pressing it against brood patch with its feet. After hatching, male tends young for several weeks. Many are killed each year in oil spills and fishnets.

female pg. 187

male

Greater Scaup
Aythya marila

MIGRATION
SUMMER

Size: 18" (45 cm)

Male: A mostly black and white duck. Black head shines green in direct sunlight. Bright white sides and a gray back. Light blue bill with a black tip. Rounded head.

Female: brown with a darker head and a bold white patch at the base of bill, might show a white patch behind each eye, rounded top of head

Juvenile: same as female

Nest: ground; female builds; 1 brood per year

Eggs: 7-10; greenish olive without markings

Incubation: 24-28 days; female incubates

Fledging: 45-50 days; female teaches young to feed

Migration: complete, to western coastal U.S., Mexico

Food: aquatic plants and insects

Compare: Male Lesser Scaup (pg. 51) is very similar, but male Greater Scaup is slightly larger, has a more rounded head and a larger black mark on the tip of bill. The male Common Goldeneye (pg. 67) has a white chest and a distinctive white mark in front of each eye. The male Canvasback (pg. 329) is larger and has a red head and neck.

Stan's Notes: Common summer resident and migrant, breeding in the southern two-thirds of Alaska. More common than the Lesser Scaup, but before 1920, the Lesser Scaup was more common. Most abundant on large saltwater bays.

winter
pg. 185

breeding

Red-necked Grebe
Podiceps grisegena

Size: 18" (45 cm)

Male: Breeding (Feb-Aug) has a bold black and white pattern on the head, a rusty red neck and brown body. Long thin bill with yellow lower mandible and dark upper.

Female: same as male

Juvenile: similar to winter adult

Nest: floating platform; female and male build; 1 brood per year

Eggs: 3-6; white without markings

Incubation: 21-23 days; female and male incubate

Fledging: 50-70 days; female and male feed young

Migration: complete to non-migrator in Alaska

Food: aquatic insects, small fish

Compare: The breeding Common Loon (pg. 79) has a checkered back. Breeding Common Murre (pg. 57) has a dark head and neck.

Stan's Notes: One of seven grebe species in North America. Like the other grebes, it has a tiny tail that is usually hidden in its fluffy feathers at the base of tail (coverts). It has lobed toes unlike ducks, which have webbed feet. Found in small ponds and shallow lakes lined with reeds and sedges. Forages for food by diving for aquatic insects, often remaining underwater for up to a minute. Doesn't fly much once at nesting grounds. Builds a floating nest with plants and anchors it to one spot. Floating keeps nest from submerging when water rises during spring snowmelt. Young hatch one day at a time. Parents feed the young tiny feathers. This presumably helps protect the stomach lining from bones in fish, its main diet.

female
pg. 193

male

YEAR-ROUND
SUMMER
WINTER

Barrow's Goldeneye
Bucephala islandica

Size: 18-20" (45-50 cm)

Male: A black and white duck with a large puffy head. Head appears deep green in bright sunlight. Top of head is low and flat. Bright golden eyes. A large crescent-shaped white mark in front of each eye. Small dark bill.

Female: large dark brown head, gray body, golden eyes, small mostly yellow bill, white collar

Juvenile: same as female, but has a dark bill

Nest: cavity; female lines old woodpecker cavity; 1 brood per year

Eggs: 9-11; green to olive without markings

Incubation: 32-34 days; female incubates

Fledging: 55-60 days; female leads young to food

Migration: partial to non-migrator, to southern coastal Alaska and western coastal states

Food: aquatic insects and plants, mollusks

Compare: Male Common Goldeneye (pg. 67) has a round white spot in front of each eye and a tall, almost peaked top of head. Look for a white crescent mark in front of each eye.

Stan's Notes: Nests in cavities near ponds and lakes. Will also use a nest box. Female often returns to the same nest location for many years. Female may mate with the same male from year to year. Male leaves female once she starts incubating. Young remain in the nest 24-36 hours before fledging. Often swims out to open water when threatened instead of flying away. Will hybridize with the closely related Common Goldeneye, producing a bird with a maroon head.

male

female pg. 195

SUMMER
WINTER

Common Goldeneye
Bucephala clangula

Size: 18½-20" (47-50 cm)

Male: A mostly white duck with a black back and large, puffy green head. Large white spot in front of each bright golden eye. Dark bill.

Female: large dark brown head, gray body, white collar, bright golden eyes, yellow-tipped dark bill

Juvenile: same as female, but has a dark bill

Nest: cavity; female lines old woodpecker cavity; 1 brood per year

Eggs: 8-10; light green without markings

Incubation: 28-32 days; female incubates

Fledging: 56-59 days; female leads young to food

Migration: complete, to southern coastal Alaska, western states and Mexico

Food: aquatic plants, insects, fish, mollusks

Compare: The male Barrow's Goldeneye (pg. 65) has a white crescent mark in front of each eye. The male Greater Scaup (pg. 61) and Lesser Scaup (pg. 51) are similar, but smaller. Look for the white chest and round white spot in front of each golden eye.

Stan's Notes: Known for its loud whistling, produced by its wings in flight. In late winter and early spring, male often attracts female through elaborate displays, throwing its head backward while it utters a single raspy note. Female will lay eggs in other goldeneye nests, which results in some mothers incubating up to 30 eggs. Received the common name from its obvious bright golden eyes.

in flight

male

female pg. 199

MIGRATION
SUMMER
WINTER

Surf Scoter
Melanitta perspicillata

Size: 20" (50 cm)

Male: Black duck with a white patch on forehead and nape of neck. Large multicolored bill with a white base, black spot and orange tip. Bright white eyes.

Female: brown duck with a dark crown, white mark on nape, vertical white patch at the base of a large dark bill, bright white eyes

Juvenile: similar to female

Nest: ground; female builds; 1 brood per year

Eggs: 5-8; light pink to buff without markings

Incubation: 30-31 days; female incubates

Fledging: 45-50 days; female feeds young

Migration: complete, to southern coastal Alaska, western coastal U.S. and Mexico

Food: mollusks, crustaceans, aquatic insects

Compare: The male Black Scoter (pg. 13) has a yellow knob on its bill and lacks white patches on head. Male White-winged Scoter (pg. 15) has a white patch underneath each eye and a smaller, bicolored yellow and orange bill.

Stan's Notes: Dives or scoots through breaking surf. However, the common name "Scoter" may refer to the sooty black color of its plumage. Dives down to 40 feet (12 m) in seawater, foraging for mussels and crustaceans. Fish eggs make up 90 percent of its diet during spring and early summer. Nests on the tundra in Alaska near freshwater lakes and ponds. Spends the winter at sea, rarely returning to shore. Sometimes in mixed flocks with other scoters.

Black-billed Magpie
Pica hudsonia

YEAR-ROUND

Size: 20" (50 cm)

Male: A large black-and-white bird with very long tail and white belly. Iridescent green wings and tail in direct sunlight. Large black bill and legs. White wing patches flash in flight.

Female: same as male

Juvenile: same as adult, but has a shorter tail

Nest: modified pendulous; the female and male build; 1 brood per year

Eggs: 5-8; green with brown markings

Incubation: 16-21 days; female incubates

Fledging: 25-29 days; female and male feed young

Migration: non-migrator

Food: insects, carrion, fruit, seeds

Compare: Contrasting black-and-white colors and the very long tail of Magpie distinguish it from the all-black Northwestern Crow (pg. 9).

Stan's Notes: A wonderfully intelligent bird that is able to mimic dogs, cats and even people. Will often raid a barnyard dog dish for food. Feeds on a variety of food from road kill to insects and seeds it collects from the ground. Easily identified by its bold black-and-white colors and long streaming tail. Travels in small flocks, usually family members, and tends to be very gregarious. Breeds in small colonies. Unusual dome nest (dome-shaped roof) deep within thick shrubs. Mates with same mate for several years. Prefers open fields with cattle or sheep, where it feeds on insects attracted to livestock.

soaring

Osprey
Pandion haliaetus

Size: 24" (60 cm); up to 5½-foot wingspan

Male: Large eagle-like bird with a white chest and belly, and a nearly black back. White head with a black streak through the eyes. Large wings with black "wrist" marks. Dark bill.

Female: same as male, but larger with a necklace of brown streaking

Juvenile: similar to adults, with a light tan breast

Nest: platform, often on raised wooden platform; female and male build; 1 brood per year

Eggs: 2-4; white with brown markings

Incubation: 32-42 days; female and male incubate

Fledging: 48-58 days; male and female feed young

Migration: complete, to southern states, Mexico and Central and South America

Food: fish

Compare: Bald Eagle (pg. 81) is on average 10 inches (25 cm) larger with an all-white head and tail. The juvenile Bald Eagle is brown with white speckles. Look for a white belly and dark stripe through eyes to identify Osprey.

Stan's Notes: Ospreys are in a family all their own. It is the only raptor that plunges into water feet first to catch fish. Can hover for a few seconds before diving. Carries fish in a head-first position for better aerodynamics. Often harassed by Bald Eagles for its catch. In flight, wings are angled (cocked) backward. Nests on man-made towers and in tall dead trees. Studies show Ospreys mate for a long time, perhaps for life. May not migrate to same wintering grounds.

female pg. 221

male

YEAR-ROUND
SUMMER
WINTER

Common Eider
Somateria mollissima

Size: 24" (60 cm)

Male: Black and white duck with a large body and short neck. Long forehead slopes into a large yellow bill. Black cap, concealing dark eyes. Often has a green wash to nape of neck.

Female: smaller than male, brown with a gray bill

Juvenile: similar to female

Nest: ground; female builds; 1 brood per year

Eggs: 3-6; pale green without markings

Incubation: 25-30 days; female incubates

Fledging: 65-75 days; female leads young to food

Migration: partial to non-migrator

Food: aquatic insects

Compare: The large size, unique shape and forehead sloping into a large yellow bill make this duck easy to identify. Look for a heavy body and broad wings during flight.

Stan's Notes: This is our largest sea duck. Found along the Pacific and Atlantic coasts. The western Arctic variety has a yellow bill, while the eastern variety has a green bill. Nests in small colonies on tundra ponds and rocky shores, usually within 100 feet (30 m) of water. Often prefers to nest on small islands that lack mammalian populations, especially Arctic Foxes. Mates may stay together for several years, but the male will leave the female shortly after she begins to incubate. Mothers usually don't eat while incubating, but leave to feed, regaining lost body fat after the young fledge. Two or three groups of ducklings gathered together (crèches) are tended by 1-2 older females.

in flight

Brant
Branta bernicla

MIGRATION
SUMMER
WINTER

Size: 25" (63 cm); up to 3½-foot wingspan

Male: A large black and white goose. Black head and neck with a small white necklace just under the chin. Small dark bill. Belly ranges from light gray to black. White rump and tail. Black edge of tail. Black legs and feet.

Female: same as male

Juvenile: similar to adult by its first summer

Nest: ground; female builds; 1 brood per year

Eggs: 4-8; pale white without markings

Incubation: 22-26 days; female incubates

Fledging: 40-50 days; female and male lead the young to food

Migration: complete, to western coastal U.S., Mexico

Food: aquatic insects, grasses, sedges, moss, seeds, lichen

Compare: Smaller than Greater White-fronted Goose (pg. 223), which lacks the dark head, neck and white necklace. Similar size as Canada Goose (pg. 303), which has a white cheek patch. Look for the Brant's white necklace.

Stan's Notes: A coastal goose, almost always in flocks on shallow bays, river deltas and marshes. Flocks fly in irregular V shapes with other goose species. Nearly half nest on the Yukon-Kuskokwim Delta; the rest nest farther north along coastal Alaska. Usually nests in shallow depressions lined with seaweed and down from mother. Mother covers her eggs with downy feathers when not incubating.

winter

breeding

YEAR-ROUND
SUMMER

Common Loon
Gavia immer

Size: 28-36" (71-90 cm)

Male: Breeding adult has a black-and-white back with a checkerboard pattern, a black head, white necklace, deep red eyes and a long, pointed black bill. Winter adult has an all-gray body and bill.

Female: same as male

Juvenile: similar to winter adult, lacks red eyes

Nest: platform, on the ground; female and male build; 1 brood per year

Eggs: 2; olive brown, occasionally brown markings

Incubation: 26-31 days; female and male incubate

Fledging: 75-80 days; female and male feed young

Migration: complete to non-migrator in Alaska

Food: fish, aquatic insects

Compare: The breeding Red-throated Loon (pg. 299) has a red throat. Double-crested Cormorant (pg. 21) has a black chest and gray bill with yellow at the base and a hooked tip.

Stan's Notes: A true symbol of the wildness of our lakes. Prefers clear lakes because it hunts for fish by eyesight. Legs are set so far back that it has a difficult time walking on land, but it is a great swimmer. The common name comes from the Swedish word *lom*, meaning "lame," for the awkward way it walks on land. Its unique call suggests the wild laughter of a demented person and led to the phrase "crazy as a loon." Young ride on backs of swimming parents. Adults perform distraction displays to protect young. Very sensitive to disturbance during nesting and will abandon nest.

soaring

juvenile

soaring
juvenile

Bald Eagle
Haliaeetus leucocephalus

YEAR-ROUND
SUMMER

Size: 31-37" (79-94 cm); up to 7-foot wingspan

Male: Pure white head and tail contrast with dark brown-to-black body and wings. A large, curved yellow bill and yellow feet.

Female: same as male, only slightly larger

Juvenile: dark brown with white spots or speckles throughout body and wings, gray bill

Nest: massive platform, usually in a tree; female and male build; 1 brood per year

Eggs: 2; off-white without markings

Incubation: 34-36 days; female and male incubate

Fledging: 75-90 days; female and male feed young

Migration: partial to non-migrator; will move around to find food

Food: fish, carrion, birds (mainly ducks)

Compare: Golden Eagle (pg. 225) lacks the white head and white tail of adult Bald Eagle. Juvenile Golden Eagle, with its white "wrist" marks and white base of tail, is similar to juvenile Bald Eagle.

Stan's Notes: Driven to near extinction due to DDT poisoning and illegal killing. Now making a comeback in North America. Returns to same nest each year, adding more sticks, enlarging it to massive proportions, at times up to 1,000 pounds (450 kg). In the midair mating ritual, one eagle will flip upside down and lock talons with another. Both tumble, then break apart to continue flight. Thought to mate for life, but will switch mates if not successful reproducing. Juvenile attains the white head and tail at about 4-5 years of age.

SUMMER

Tree Swallow
Tachycineta bicolor

Size: 5-6" (13-15 cm)

Male: Blue green during spring and greener in fall. Appears to change color in direct sunlight. White chin, breast and belly. Long, pointed wing tips. Notched tail.

Female: similar to male, only duller

Juvenile: gray brown with a white belly and grayish breast band

Nest: cavity; female and male line former woodpecker cavity or nest box; 1 brood per year

Eggs: 4-6; white without markings

Incubation: 13-16 days; female incubates

Fledging: 20-24 days; female and male feed young

Migration: complete, to Mexico and Central America

Food: insects

Compare: The Barn Swallow (pg. 85) has a rust belly and deeply forked tail. The Bank Swallow (pg. 99) has a breast band and lacks the Tree Swallow's iridescent blue green colors. The Cliff Swallow (pg. 101) is a similar size and has a unique tan-to-rust color pattern.

Stan's Notes: The first swallow species to return each spring. Most common at coastal beaches, ponds, lakes and agricultural fields. Will compete with bluebirds for cavities and nesting boxes. Can be attracted to your yard with a nesting box. Travels great distances to find dropped feathers to line its grass nest. Sometimes seen playing, chasing after dropped feathers. Often seen flying back and forth across fields, feeding on insects. Gathers in large flocks to migrate.

SUMMER

Barn Swallow
Hirundo rustica

Size: 7" (18 cm)

Male: A sleek swallow. Blue black back, cinnamon belly and reddish brown chin. White spots on a long, deeply forked tail.

Female: same as male, only slightly duller

Juvenile: similar to adults, with a tan belly and chin and a shorter tail

Nest: cup; female and male construct; 2 broods per year

Eggs: 4-5; white with brown markings

Incubation: 13-17 days; female incubates

Fledging: 18-23 days; female and male feed young

Migration: complete, to South America

Food: insects, prefers beetles, wasps and flies

Compare: The Tree Swallow (pg. 83) has a white belly and chin and a notched tail. Bank Swallow (pg. 99) lacks the cinnamon belly and blue black back. The Cliff Swallow (pg. 101) and Violet-green Swallow (pg. 307) are smaller and lack the distinctive, deeply forked tail. Violet-green Swallow has a white face.

Stan's Notes: Five regularly occurring swallow species in Alaska; this is the only one with a deeply forked tail. Unlike other swallows, Barn Swallows rarely glide in flight, so look for continuous flapping. Builds a mud nest using up to 1,000 beak-loads of mud, often in or on barns. Nests in colonies of 4-6 individuals, but nesting alone is not uncommon. Drinks in flight, skimming water or getting water from wet leaves. Also bathes while flying through rain or sprinklers.

Mountain Bluebird
Sialia currucoides

Size: 7" (18 cm)

Male: An overall sky blue bird with a darker blue head, back, wings and tail and white lower belly. Thin black bill.

Female: similar to male, but paler with a nearly gray head and chest and a whitish belly

Juvenile: similar to adult of the same sex

Nest: cavity, old woodpecker cavity, wooden nest box; female builds; 1-2 broods per year

Eggs: 4-6; pale blue without markings

Incubation: 13-14 days; female incubates

Fledging: 22-23 days; female and male feed young

Migration: complete, to southwestern states, Mexico

Food: insects, fruit

Compare: Larger than Bluethroat (pg. 241), which is gray with blue only around the area of the throat. Look for male Mountain Bluebird's dark blue head, back and wings.

Stan's Notes: Found in open mountainous country. Feeds mainly on insects, but will also eat fruit. Often hovers just before diving to the ground to grab an insect. Hovers at nest cavity entrance. Due to conservation of suitable nesting sites (dead trees with cavities and man-made nest boxes), populations have increased over the past 30 years. Like other bluebirds, Mountain Bluebirds take well to nest boxes and tolerate close contact with humans. Female continues to sit on baby birds (brood) for up to six days after eggs hatch. Young imprint on their first nest box or cavity, then choose a similar type of box or cavity throughout the rest of life.

YEAR-ROUND

Steller's Jay
Cyanocitta stelleri

Size: 11" (28 cm)

Male: Dark blue wings, tail and belly. Black head, nape and breast. Large, pointed black crest that can be lifted at will.

Female: same as male

Juvenile: similar to adult

Nest: cup; female and male construct; 1 brood per year

Eggs: 3-5; pale green with brown markings

Incubation: 14-16 days; female incubates

Fledging: 16-18 days; female and male feed young

Migration: non-migrator

Food: insects, berries, seeds; will visit seed feeders

Compare: The Gray Jay (pg. 279) is slightly larger and lacks any blue and a crest. Belted Kingfisher (pg. 91) is larger, lacks the black head and has a less prominent crest.

Stan's Notes: Named after Arctic explorer Georg W. Steller, who is said to have discovered the bird on the Alaskan coast in 1741. A year-round resident of foothills and lower mountains in southeastern Alaska. Usually seen in coniferous forests. Rarely competes with Gray Jays, which occupy higher elevations. Thought to mate for life. Will rarely disperse very far, often breeding within 10 miles (16 km) of its birthplace. Several subspecies seen in the U.S. West. The Alaska form (shown) has a black crest and lacks any distinct white streaks on head.

YEAR-ROUND
SUMMER
WINTER

Belted Kingfisher
Ceryle alcyon

Size: 13" (33 cm)

Male: Large blue bird with white belly. Broad blue gray breast band and a ragged crest that is raised and lowered at will. Large head with a long, thick black bill. A small white spot directly in front of red brown eyes. Black wing tips with splashes of white that flash when flying.

Female: same as male, but with rusty breast band in addition to blue gray band, and rusty flanks

Juvenile: similar to female

Nest: cavity; female and male excavate; 1 brood per year

Eggs: 6-7; white without markings

Incubation: 23-24 days; female and male incubate

Fledging: 23-24 days; female and male feed young

Migration: complete to non-migrator in Alaska

Food: small fish

Compare: Larger than the Steller's Jay (pg. 89), which has a black head and more prominent crest. Gray Jay (pg. 279) lacks the breast band of the Belted Kingfisher.

Stan's Notes: Seen perched on branches close to water, it will dive headfirst for small fish and returns to a branch to eat. Has a loud machine-gun-like call. Excavates a deep cavity in bank of river or lake. Parents drop dead fish into water, teaching the young to dive. Regurgitates pellets of bone after meals, being unable to pass bones through the digestive tract. Mates recognize each other by call.

YEAR-ROUND

Chestnut-backed Chickadee
Poecile rufescens

Size: 4¾" (12 cm)

Male: Rich, warm chestnut back and sides. Black crown and chin. White cheeks and sides of head. Gray wings and tail.

Female: same as male

Juvenile: same as adult

Nest: cavity; female and male build; 1-2 broods per year

Eggs: 5-7; white without markings

Incubation: 10-12 days; female incubates

Fledging: 13-16 days; female and male feed young

Migration: non-migrator

Food: insects, seeds, fruit; comes to seed and suet feeders

Compare: Black-capped Chickadee (pg. 233) and Boreal Chickadee (pg. 235) lack Chestnut-backed's distinctive chestnut back.

Stan's Notes: The most colorful of all chickadees. Like the other chickadee species, the Chestnut-backed clings to branches upside down, looking for insects. During breeding, it is quiet and secretive. In winter it joins other birds such as kinglets, woodpeckers and other chickadees. Prefers humid coniferous forests. Builds a cavity nest 2-20 feet (up to 6 m) above the ground. Will use the same nest year after year. Visits seed and suet feeders.

male

Hoary Redpoll

female

YEAR-ROUND
SUMMER
WINTER

Common Redpoll
Carduelis flammea

Size: 5" (13 cm)

Male: A small sparrow-like ˘ crown and black spot on the chin. Heavily streaked back and a splash of raspberry red on the chest.

Female: same as male, but lacking raspberry red on the chest

Juvenile: browner than adults, lacks a red crown, has dark streaks on the chest

Nest: cup; female builds; 1 brood (sometimes 2) per year

Eggs: 4-5; pale green with purple markings

Incubation: 10-11 days; female incubates

Fledging: 11-12 days; female and male feed young

Migration: irruptive; moves around in groups during winter to find food

Food: seeds, insects; will come to seed feeders

Compare: Smaller than Snow Bunting (pg. 25), which lacks a red crown. Same size as Pine Siskin (pg. 97), which has yellow wing bars and lacks the red crown. Look for the bright red crown and black spot under the bill.

Stan's Notes: Name is derived from the color and "taking a poll" or counting heads. Seen throughout Alaska. Winter flocks of up to 100 birds are not uncommon. Bathes in snow when water is not available. Much like Black-capped Chickadees, it can be tamed and hand fed. Hoary Redpoll (see inset) is overall paler than Common Redpoll with less streaking on flanks and a pink wash on breast.

YEAR-ROUND
SUMMER

Pine Siskin
Carduelis pinus

Size: 5" (13 cm)

Male: Small brown finch. Heavily streaked back, breast and belly. Yellow wing bars. Yellow at base of tail. Thin bill.

Female: same as male

Juvenile: similar to adult, light yellow tinge over the breast and chin

Nest: modified cup; female constructs; 2 broods per year

Eggs: 3-4; greenish blue with brown markings

Incubation: 12-13 days; female incubates

Fledging: 14-15 days; female and male feed young

Migration: irruptive; moves around the U.S. in search of food

Food: seeds, insects; will come to seed feeders

Compare: Same size as the Common Redpoll (pg. 95), which has a red crown and black spot on the chin. Look for the Pine Siskin's streaked breast and yellow wing bars to help identify.

Stan's Notes: A nesting resident in southeastern parts of Alaska. Usually considered a winter finch. More visible in the non-nesting season, when it gathers in flocks, moves around and visits feeders. Comes to thistle feeders. Travels and breeds in small groups. Male feeds female during incubation. Juveniles lose their yellow tint by late summer of the first year. Constructs its nest toward the ends of coniferous branches, where needles are dense, helping to conceal. Nests are often only a few feet apart.

Bank Swallow
Riparia riparia

Size: 5¼" (13 cm)

Male: A dull brown-to-gray swallow with a white chin and belly contrasting against a brown breast band. Long pointed wings. Tiny dark bill. Small legs and feet.

Female: same as male

Juvenile: similar to adult, but has a white chin and white extending behind eyes

Nest: cavity; female and male excavate; 1 brood per year

Eggs: 3-7; white without markings

Incubation: 14-16 days; female and male incubate

Fledging: 18-24 days, female and male feed young

Migration: complete, to South America

Food: insects

Compare: The Tree Swallow (pg. 83) is iridescent blue green and lacks a breast band. Cliff Swallow (pg. 101) has a tan-to-rust rump, cheeks and forehead. Barn Swallow (pg. 85) has a blue black back and cinnamon belly.

Stan's Notes: A colony swallow that excavates its nest cavity in a riverbank. Nest cavities are often 2-3 feet (up to 1 m) deep and have a feather lining in the nest chamber. Known to use an old Kingfisher nest cavity. Mated pairs will pass a feather back and forth while in flight to strengthen the bond between them. Entire colony tends to breed at the same time (synchronously). Members of the colony lead others to food sources. After young fledge, the colony gathers in extremely large flocks for roosting just before migrating.

SUMMER

Cliff Swallow
Petrochelidon pyrrhonota

Size: 5½" (14 cm)

Male: A uniquely patterned swallow with a dark back, wings and cap. Distinctive tan-to-rust rump, cheeks and forehead.

Female: same as male

Juvenile: similar to adult, lacks distinct patterning

Nest: gourd-shaped, made of mud; the male and female build; 1-2 broods per year

Eggs: 3-6; pale white with brown markings

Incubation: 14-16 days; male and female incubate

Fledging: 21-24 days; female and male feed young

Migration: complete, to South America

Food: insects

Compare: Smaller than Barn Swallow (pg. 85), which has a distinctive, deeply forked tail and blue back and wings. Bank Swallow (pg. 99) is a similar size and lacks the unique tan-to-rust coloring on the rump, cheeks and forehead.

Stan's Notes: Summer resident in parts of Alaska. Common around bridges (especially bridges over water) and rural housing (especially in open country near cliffs). Constructs a gourd-shaped nest with a funnel-like entrance pointing down. A colony nester, with many nests lined up beneath eaves of buildings or under cliff overhangs. Will carry balls of mud up to a mile to construct its nest. Many of the colony return to the same nest sites each year. Not unusual to have two broods per season. If the number of nests beneath eaves becomes a problem, wait until after the young have left the nests to hose off the mud.

male pg. 237

female

SUMMER

Dark-eyed Junco
Junco hyemalis

Size: 5½" (14 cm)

Female: Round, dark-eyed bird with a tan-to-brown chest, head and back. White belly. Ivory-to-pink bill. Since the outermost tail feathers are white, tail appears as a white V in flight.

Male: same as female, only slate gray to charcoal

Juvenile: similar to female, but has a streaked breast and head

Nest: cup; female and male construct, 2 broods per year

Eggs: 3-5; white with reddish brown markings

Incubation: 12-13 days; female incubates

Fledging: 10-13 days; male and female feed young

Migration: complete, throughout the U.S.

Food: seeds, insects; will come to seed feeders

Compare: Rarely confused with any other bird. The Dark-eyed Junco is not in Alaska during the winter.

Stan's Notes: This is one of Alaska's common summer birds. Nests in a wide variety of wooded habitats in April and May. Adheres to a rigid social hierarchy, with dominant birds chasing less dominant birds. Look for its white outer tail feathers flashing while in flight. Most comfortable on the ground, juncos will "double-scratch" with both feet to expose seeds and insects. Consumes many weed seeds. Usually seen on the ground in small flocks. Females tend to migrate farther south than the males. Several junco species have now been combined into one, simply called Dark-eyed Junco.

SUMMER

Savannah Sparrow
Passerculus sandwichensis

Size: 5½" (14 cm)

Male: Overall brown bird with fine streaks on the breast and a central dark spot. White belly and chin. Distinctive stripe down center of crown. Dark line extending from the back of each eye and from the base of bill to back of head. Yellowish eyebrows. Small bill.

Female: same as male

Juvenile: similar to adult

Nest: cup; female builds; 1-2 broods per year

Eggs: 3-5; pale green to white, brown markings

Incubation: 10-13 days; female incubates

Fledging: 10-14 days; female and male feed young

Migration: complete, to southwestern states, Mexico

Food: seeds, insects

Compare: The Song Sparrow (pg. 107) is not as widespread and has coarse brown streaks on its breast compared with the fine streaks of the Savannah Sparrow. The Golden-crowned Sparrow (pg. 123) is larger and has a black and yellow crown.

Stan's Notes: Common sparrow of various habitats. Sometimes in small flocks. Many geographical variations, ranging from very pale brown and gray to dark brown to nearly black. In Alaska, most are medium brown. Often runs across the ground like a mouse. Some males mate with several females (polygamous). May nest in small groups. Lines nest with moss, grass and hair. Nest is usually flush with the ground in a natural or excavated depression.

Song Sparrow
Melospiza melodia

YEAR-ROUND

Size: 5-6" (13-15 cm)

Male: Common brown sparrow with heavy dark streaks on breast coalescing into a central dark spot.

Female: same as male

Juvenile: similar to adult, finely streaked breast, lacks a central spot

Nest: cup; female builds; 2 broods per year

Eggs: 3-4; pale blue to green with reddish brown markings

Incubation: 12-14 days; female incubates

Fledging: 9-12 days; female and male feed young

Migration: non-migrator to partial

Food: insects, seeds; rarely visits seed feeders

Compare: Similar to other brown sparrows. Savannah Sparrow (pg. 105) is more widespread and has fine brown streaks on its breast. Look for Song Sparrow's heavily streaked breast.

Stan's Notes: Many subspecies or varieties of Song Sparrow, but the dark central spot is found in each variant. Returns to a similar area each year, defending a small territory by singing from thick shrubs. This is a constant songster that repeats its loud, clear song every couple minutes. Song varies in structure, but is basically the same from region to region. A ground feeder, look for it to scratch at the same time with both feet ("double-scratch") to expose seeds. While the female builds another nest for a second brood, the male often takes over feeding the young. Unlike many other sparrow species, Song Sparrows rarely flock together.

side view

front view

American Tree Sparrow
Spizella arborea

Size: 6" (15 cm)

Male: Common brown sparrow with a tan breast and rusty crown. Black spot in the center of breast. Upper bill is dark, lower bill yellow. Two white wing bars. Gray eyebrows.

Female: same as male

Juvenile: lacks a rust crown, has a streaked chest that often obscures the central dark spot

Nest: cup; female builds; 1 brood per year

Eggs: 3-5; green white with brown markings

Incubation: 12-13 days; female incubates

Fledging: 8-10 days; female and male feed young

Migration: complete, throughout North America

Food: insects, seeds; visits seed feeders

Compare: Appears similar to other sparrow species. Song Sparrow (pg. 107) has a similar size and a heavily streaked breast. Look closely at the breast for a single dark spot in the center and no streaking to help identify the American Tree Sparrow.

Stan's Notes: Bird feeder visitor in Alaska during summer. Breeds throughout the state. Seen mostly during migration in flocks that range from 2-200. The species name *arborea* means "tree," but it doesn't nest in trees. Nests on the ground in a clump or tuft of grass (tussock). The common name "Tree Sparrow" refers to its habitat. "American" refers to its natural range.

Gray-crowned Rosy-Finch
Leucosticte tephrocotis

YEAR-ROUND
SUMMER

Size: 6" (15 cm)

Male: Gray crown with a black forehead, chin and throat. Warm cinnamon brown body with a wash of rosy red, especially along flanks and rump.

Female: same as male, but has less pink

Juvenile: similar to adult of the same sex

Nest: cup; female builds; 1-2 broods per year

Eggs: 3-5; white without markings

Incubation: 12-14 days; female incubates

Fledging: 16-18 days; female and male feed young

Migration: complete to partial migrator in Alaska

Food: seeds, insects; will visit seed feeders

Compare: Slightly larger than the female Dark-eyed Junco (pg. 103), but has a gray crown, rosy red flanks and dark belly. Lapland Longspur (pg. 119) is slightly larger and has a rusty red nape.

Stan's Notes: Seen in high alpine regions. Breeds throughout most of Alaska. Moves into southern coastal parts of the state in winter. Almost always seen in small flocks, foraging on the ground near patches of snow in high elevations. Nests in steep cliff faces. During breeding, both male and female develop an opening in the floor of the mouth (buccal pouch), which is used to carry a large supply of food to young in nest. Comes to feeders offering sunflower seeds.

MIGRATION
SUMMER

Northern Waterthrush
Seiurus noveboracensis

Size: 6" (15 cm)

Male: A large, overall dark brown warbler. Chest, chin and belly are white to pale yellow with heavy dark streaks. Long narrow eyebrows, white to pale yellow, extending from base of bill to back of head.

Female: same as male

Juvenile: similar to adult

Nest: cup; female builds; 1 brood per year

Eggs: 3-6; pale white with brown markings

Incubation: 10-13 days; female incubates

Fledging: 10-11 days; female and male feed young

Migration: complete, to Mexico, Central America and South America

Food: insects, crustaceans, tiny fish, mollusks

Compare: Larger than Arctic Warbler (pg. 231), which shares light eyebrows, but lacks the heavy brown streaking of Northern Waterthrush. The Blackpoll Warbler (pg. 23) is slightly smaller and lacks light eyebrows.

Stan's Notes: One of the wood warblers. Found along woodland streams and creeks, where it hunts for insects. Spends much of its time walking along stream banks or wading in shallow water, often flipping leaves, looking for insects to eat. Constructs its nest under roots, rock shelves and overhanging banks near the water's edge. Constantly bobs head and pumps tail up and down while walking, hunting or just after landing.

non-breeding
pg. 247

breeding

MIGRATION
SUMMER

Least Sandpiper
Calidris minutilla

Size: 6" (15 cm)

Male: Breeding plumage has a golden brown head and back. White eyebrows and belly. Dull yellow legs. Short, down-curved black bill.

Female: same as male

Juvenile: similar to non-breeding adult, but is buffy brown and lacks the breast band

Nest: ground; male and female construct; 1 brood per year

Eggs: 3-4; olive with dark markings

Incubation: 19-23 days; male and female incubate

Fledging: 25-28 days; male and female feed young

Migration: complete, to California, Mexico and Central America

Food: aquatic and terrestrial insects, seeds

Compare: Often confused with the breeding Western Sandpiper (pg. 117). The Least Sandpiper's yellow legs differentiate it from other tiny sandpipers. The short, thin, down-curved bill also helps to identify.

Stan's Notes: The smallest of the peeps (sandpipers). This is a tame bird that can be approached without scaring. Nests on the Alaskan tundra. Seen in the southern three-quarters of the state in summer and during migration. Prefers the grassy flats of saltwater and freshwater ponds. The yellow legs can be hard to see in water, poor light or when covered with mud.

non-breeding
pg. 249

breeding

MIGRATION
SUMMER

Western Sandpiper
Calidris mauri

Size: 6½" (16 cm)

Male: Breeding has a bright rust brown crown, ear patch and back and a white chin and chest. Black legs. Narrow bill that droops near tip.

Female: same as male

Juvenile: similar to breeding adult, bright buff brown on the back only

Nest: ground; male and female construct; 1 brood per year

Eggs: 2-4; light brown with dark markings

Incubation: 20-22 days; male and female incubate

Fledging: 19-21 days; male and female feed young

Migration: complete, to California, Mexico and Central America

Food: aquatic and terrestrial insects

Compare: Breeding Least Sandpiper (pg. 115) lacks the black legs and bright rusty brown cap, ear patch and back. Western has a longer bill that droops slightly at the tip. Breeding Red Knot (pg. 327) lacks the rusty brown back and white belly.

Stan's Notes: Summer resident along the western coast of Alaska, nesting on the tundra in large "loose" colonies. Feeds on insects at the water's edge, sometimes immersing its head. Young leave the nest (precocial) within a few hours after hatching. Female leaves and the male tends the hatchlings. A long-distance migrant, with adults leaving the breeding grounds several weeks before young.

male

non-breeding male

female

MIGRATION
SUMMER

Lapland Longspur
Calcarius lapponicus

Size: 6½" (16 cm)

Male: Overall brown with a black head, throat and chest. Tan eyebrows. Rusty red nape. White belly. Small, pointed yellow bill with a black tip. Non-breeding plumage is much duller. Lacks the black head, throat and chest.

Female: very similar to non-breeding male

Juvenile: similar to female, but duller

Nest: cup; female builds; 1 brood per year

Eggs: 3-7; pale green with brown markings

Incubation: 12-13 days; female incubates

Fledging: 8-10 days; male and female feed young

Migration: complete, to northwestern states

Food: insects, seeds

Compare: The Gray-crowned Rosy-Finch (pg. 111) is slightly smaller and lacks a rusty red nape. Breeding male Snow Bunting (pg. 25) has a white head. Look for the black head to help identify the breeding male Lapland.

Stan's Notes: One of four longspur species in North America. A summer resident and migrator in Alaska, often seen in open areas and along roads. Usually found in flocks with Horned Larks and Snow Buntings. Common name "Longspur" refers to the long rear toe and nail, which are nearly twice the length of the front two toes. Has one of the widest breeding ranges, extending around the world just south of the polar region (circumpolar). Breeding plumage is seen from March to September. Builds nest in a shallow depression on the ground.

juvenile

SUMMER

White-crowned Sparrow
Zonotrichia leucophrys

Size: 6½-7½" (16-19 cm)

Male: A brown sparrow with a gray breast and a black-and-white striped crown. Small, thin pink bill.

Female: same as male

Juvenile: similar to adult, with brown stripes on the head instead of white

Nest: cup; female builds; 2 broods per year

Eggs: 3-5; color varies from greenish to bluish to whitish with red brown markings

Incubation: 11-14 days; female incubates

Fledging: 8-12 days; male and female feed young

Migration: complete, to western coastal states, Mexico

Food: insects, seeds, berries; visits ground feeders

Compare: Golden-crowned Sparrow (pg. 123) has a central yellow spot on the crown. The Song Sparrow (pg. 107) has heavy dark streaks on the breast coalescing into a central spot.

Stan's Notes: Usually seen in groups of up to 20 during migration and summer, when it can be seen feeding underneath seed feeders. A ground feeder, scratching backward with both feet at the same time. Males arrive on breeding grounds before the females and establish territories by singing from perches. Male takes the most responsibility of raising the young while female starts the second brood. Only 9-12 days separate broods. Nests in the southern two-thirds of Alaska.

non-breeding

breeding

Golden-crowned Sparrow
Zonotrichia atricapilla

Size: 7" (18 cm)

Male: All-brown sparrow with a heavy body, long tail and yellow spot in the center of a black crown. Gray around head and chest. Upper bill (mandible) is darker than the lower bill (mandible). Non-breeding adult has various amounts of black on crown.

Female: same as male

Juvenile: similar to adult, lacks the black and yellow crown

Nest: cup; female and male construct; 1 brood per year

Eggs: 3-5; bluish white with brown markings

Incubation: 10-14 days; female incubates

Fledging: 8-14 days; female and male feed young

Migration: complete, to western coastal states, Mexico

Food: insects, seeds, berries

Compare: The White-crowned Sparrow (pg. 121) is similar, but lacks the yellow patch in the center of its crown. The Savannah Sparrow (pg. 105) is smaller and lacks the black and yellow crown.

Stan's Notes: A common summer bird, breeding in the southern half of Alaska. Often seen in flocks with other sparrows. Male feeds female while she incubates. There are varying amounts of black on the head during winter, but the yellow patch remains the same.

SUMMER

Fox Sparrow
Passerella iliaca

Size: 7" (18 cm)

Male: A plump rusty sparrow. Two morphs occur in Alaska. Red morph is rusty red with a heavily streaked rusty breast and solid rust tail. Head and back are mottled with gray. Pacific variety is rusty brown with a heavily streaked rusty breast and solid rust tail.

Female: same as male of the same morph

Juvenile: same as adult of the same morph

Nest: cup; female builds; 2 broods per year

Eggs: 2-4; pale green with reddish markings

Incubation: 12-14 days; female incubates

Fledging: 10-11 days; female and male feed young

Migration: complete, to southeastern states, western coastal states

Food: insects, seeds; comes to feeders

Compare: Rusty color differentiates the Fox Sparrow from all other sparrows. Look for a heavily streaked chest and long tail to help identify.

Stan's Notes: One of the largest sparrows. Several color variations, depending on the part of the country. Often seen only underneath seed feeders during summer and migration, searching for seeds and insects. Scratches like a chicken with both feet at the same time to find food. Usually solitary or in small groups. The common name "Sparrow" comes from the Anglo-Saxon word *spearwa*, meaning "flutterer," as applied to any small bird. "Fox" refers to the bird's rusty color. Nests on the ground in brush and at forest edges in the southern three-quarters of Alaska. Map reflects the combined range.

SUMMER

Semipalmated Plover
Charadrius semipalmatus

Size: 7" (18 cm)

Male: A brown-backed bird with a black necklace and short, black-tipped orange bill. White patch on forehead. White breast and belly. Breeding plumage has a black mask and an orange eye-ring around each eye.

Female: same as male

Juvenile: similar to adult, lacks a well-defined black necklace

Nest: ground; male builds; 1 brood per year

Eggs: 3-4; light brown with dark markings

Incubation: 23-25 days; male and female incubate

Fledging: 22-28 days; male and female feed young

Migration: complete, to western coastal U.S., Mexico

Food: insects, seeds, worms

Compare: Smaller than the Killdeer (pg. 145), which shares the brown back and white belly but has 2 black neck bands. Look for a very short bill and single black necklace to help identify the Semipalmated Plover.

Stan's Notes: A breeding bird throughout Alaska. Breeding birds usually have orange eye-rings. Hunts by running quickly, stopping to look, then stabbing prey. Prefers to nest in open rocky places, where the male will scrape out a shallow depression. Nests on the ground on the Alaskan tundra. Population decreased dramatically during the late 1800s due to hunting.

pale morph

Horned Lark
Eremophila alpestris

Size: 7-8" (18-20 cm)

Male: A sleek reddish tan bird with a yellow chin, black necklace and white lower breast and belly. Black bill. Dark tail with white outer feathers, seen in flight. Two tiny "horns" on top of head can be difficult to see.

Female: same as male, only duller, "horns" are even less noticeable

Juvenile: lacks reddish markings, black necklace and yellow chin, no "horns" until second year

Nest: ground; female builds; 2 broods per year

Eggs: 3-4; gray with brown markings

Incubation: 11-12 days; female incubates

Fledging: 9-12 days; female and male feed young

Migration: complete, to western states and Mexico

Food: seeds, insects

Compare: Slightly larger than most sparrows, with a narrow, sleeker body. Look for the black markings in front of eyes to help identify the Horned Lark.

Stan's Notes: The only true lark native to North America. Horned Larks are birds of open ground. Common in rural areas, often seen in large flocks. Population increased in North America over the past century due to land clearing for farming. Male performs a fluttering courtship flight high in the air while singing a high-pitched song. Female performs a fluttering distraction display if nest is disturbed. Can renest about a week after the brood fledges. Common name "Lark" comes from the Middle English word *laverock*, or "a lark."

non-breeding

breeding

SUMMER

Spotted Sandpiper
Actitis macularia

Size: 8" (20 cm)

Male: Olive brown back. Long bill and long dull yellow legs. White line over eyes. Breeding has black spots on a white breast and belly. Non-breeding has a clear breast and belly.

Female: same as male

Juvenile: similar to non-breeding adult, darker bill

Nest: ground; female and male build; 2 broods per year

Eggs: 3-4; brownish with brown markings

Incubation: 20-24 days; male incubates

Fledging: 17-21 days; male feeds young

Migration: complete, to southwestern states, Mexico, Central and South America

Food: aquatic insects

Compare: Smaller than Lesser Yellowlegs (pg. 141). Look for Spotted Sandpiper to bob its tail up and down while standing. Look for the breeding Spotted Sandpiper's black spots extending from breast to belly.

Stan's Notes: One of the few shorebirds that will dive underwater if pursued. Able to fly straight up out of the water. Flies with wings held in a cup-like arc, rarely lifting them above a horizontal plane. Constantly bobs its tail while standing and walks as if delicately balanced. Female mates with multiple males and lays eggs in up to five different nests. Male incubates and cares for young. Dramatic plumage change from breeding to non-breeding. Lacks black spots on the breast and belly in winter.

131

YEAR-ROUND

Northern Saw-whet Owl
Aegolius acadicus

Size: 8" (20 cm); up to 17-inch wingspan

Male: Small tawny brown owl with wide vertical rusty brown streaks on a white breast and belly. Distinctive light marks on back and wings. Short tail. A white face, yellow eyes and small dark bill.

Female: same as male

Juvenile: dark brown with a light brown belly

Nest: cavity, former woodpecker cavity; does not add any nesting material; 1 brood per year

Eggs: 5-6; white without markings

Incubation: 26-28 days; female and male incubate

Fledging: 27-34 days; male and female feed young

Migration: non-migrator in Alaska

Food: mice, small birds, insects

Compare: Great Horned Owl (pg. 217) is much larger and has large, obvious ear tufts. The Short-eared Owl (pg. 167) is nearly twice as large. Northern Hawk Owl (pg. 169) is twice as large and has a long tail.

Stan's Notes: Year-round resident in southeastern coastal Alaska. Our smallest owl, but not often recognized as an owl because of its diminutive size. Usually in coniferous-deciduous forests. Strictly a nighttime hunter. Frequently roosts in cavities in conifers or thick vegetation. Has relatively long wings for such a small raptor. The common name comes from its rarely heard call, a repeated low raspy whistle that is reminiscent of a saw blade being sharpened. Can be very tame and approachable.

Bohemian Waxwing
Bombycilla garrulus

Size: 8¼" (21 cm)

Male: Very sleek-looking bird, gray to light brown with a gray belly. Pointed crest, bandit-like black mask and black chin. Obvious yellow pattern on black wings. Wing tips look as if they were dipped in red wax. Bright yellow tip of tail and rust undertail.

Female: same as male

Juvenile: gray with a heavily streaked chest, lacks red wing tips

Nest: cup; female builds; 1 brood per year

Eggs: 4-6; pale blue with dark markings

Incubation: 13-16 days; female incubates

Fledging: 13-16 days; female and male feed young

Migration: complete to non-migrator, to the southern coast of Alaska and northern states

Food: insects, berries, fruit

Compare: Unique-looking bird, not usually confused with other species. Look for a black mask, pointed crest and rust undertail to identify.

Stan's Notes: Feather shafts in adults exude a red waxy substance. The function is unknown, but it may be a signal of sexual maturity. "Bohemian" refers to its vagabond behavior of wandering in large flocks in fall and winter. The Latin species name *garrulus* means "talkative" or "shattering" and refers to its constant vocalizations. Usually very tame and approachable. Descends upon a single tree that has fruit and remains until nearly all fruit has been consumed. Mature birds have greater nesting success than younger birds.

male pg. 5

female

Red-winged Blackbird
Agelaius phoeniceus

SUMMER

Size: 8½" (22 cm)

Female: Heavily streaked brown bird with a pointed brown bill and white eyebrows.

Male: jet black bird with red and yellow patches on upper wings, pointed black bill

Juvenile: same as female

Nest: cup; female builds; 2-3 broods per year

Eggs: 3-4; bluish green with brown markings

Incubation: 10-12 days; female incubates

Fledging: 11-14 days; female and male feed young

Migration: complete, to western states

Food: seeds, insects; will come to seed feeders

Compare: The slightly larger female Rusty Blackbird (pg. 261) lacks prominent white eyebrows and streaks on breast.

Stan's Notes: Summer resident in southeastern Alaska. It is a sure sign of spring when Red-winged Blackbirds return to the marshes. Flocks of up to 100,000 birds have been reported. Males return to Alaska before females and defend their territories by singing from the tops of surrounding vegetation. Males repeat their call from the tops of cattails while showing off their red and yellow wing bars (epaulets). Females choose a mate and will often nest over shallow water in thick stands of cattails. Red-wingeds feed mostly on seeds in fall and spring, switching to insects during summer.

non-breeding
pg. 257

breeding

MIGRATION
SUMMER

Dunlin
Calidris alpina

Size: 8-9" (20-22.5 cm)

Male: Breeding adult is distinctive with a rusty red back, finely streaked breast and an obvious black patch on the belly. Stout bill, curving slightly downward at the tip. Black legs.

Female: slightly larger than male, with a longer bill

Juvenile: slightly rusty back with a spotty breast

Nest: ground; male and female construct; 1 brood per year

Eggs: 2-4; olive buff or blue green with red brown markings

Incubation: 21-22 days; male and female incubate, male incubates during the day, female at night

Fledging: 19-21 days; male feeds young, female often leaves before young fledge

Migration: complete, to western coastal U.S., Mexico and Central America

Food: insects

Compare: Surfbird (pg. 269) and breeding Red Knot (pg. 327) are larger and lack the large black patch on belly. Look for the Dunlin's stout down-curved bill.

Stan's Notes: Breeding plumage more commonly seen in spring. Flights include heights of up to 100 feet (30 m) with brief gliding alternating with shallow flutters, and a rhythmic, repeating song. Huge flocks fly synchronously, with birds twisting and turning, flashing light and dark undersides. Males tend to fly farther south in winter than females.

MIGRATION
SUMMER

Lesser Yellowlegs
Tringa flavipes

Size: 10-11" (25-28 cm)

Male: A typical sandpiper-type bird with a brown back and wings and lightly streaked white breast and belly. Thin, straight black bill. Long yellow legs.

Female: same as male

Juvenile: same as adult

Nest: ground; female builds; 1 brood per year

Eggs: 3-4; yellowish with brown markings

Incubation: 22-23 days; male and female incubate

Fledging: 18-20 days; male and female lead young to food

Migration: complete, to South America

Food: aquatic insects, tiny fish

Compare: Greater Yellowlegs (pg. 159) has a longer, upturned bill. Breeding Spotted Sandpiper (pg. 131) has black spots on its chest.

Stan's Notes: Usually seen in small flocks, it combs shorelines and mud flats looking for aquatic insects. Most often seen in the head down, tail up position, walking along, looking to snatch up food. Uses its long straight bill to pluck insects and tiny fish from water. Very shy bird that quite often moves into the water prior to taking flight. Has a variety of "flight" notes that it gives when taking off. A member of the group of sandpipers called Tattlers, all of which scream alarm calls when taking flight. Nest is a simple depression atop a mound of earth.

non-breeding
pg. 271

breeding

MIGRATION
SUMMER

Short-billed Dowitcher
Limnodromus griseus

Size: 11" (28 cm)

Male: Breeding plumage is an overall rusty brown with heavy black spots throughout. Has a small amount of white very low on belly. A long, straight black bill. Off-white eyebrow stripe. Dull yellow-to-green legs and feet.

Female: same as male

Juvenile: similar to non-breeding adult

Nest: ground; female and male construct; 1 brood per year

Eggs: 3-4; olive green with dark markings

Incubation: 20-21 days; male and female incubate

Fledging: 25-27 days; male and female feed young

Migration: complete, to coastal Mexico

Food: insects, snails, worms, leeches, seeds

Compare: Same size as breeding Red Knot (pg. 327), which has a shorter bill and rich salmon-colored head, chest and belly. The breeding Dunlin (pg. 139) is smaller and has a black patch on belly.

Stan's Notes: Summer resident seen along southern coastal Alaska and inland on freshwater lakes and marshes. With a rapid probing action like a sewing machine, it uses its long straight bill to probe deep into sand and mud for insects.

Killdeer

Charadrius vociferus

MIGRATION
SUMMER

Size: 11" (28 cm)

Male: An upland shorebird that has 2 black bands around the neck like a necklace. A brown back and white belly. Bright reddish orange rump, visible in flight.

Female: same as male

Juvenile: similar to adult, with 1 neck band

Nest: ground; male builds; 2 broods per year

Eggs: 3-5; tan with brown markings

Incubation: 24-28 days; male and female incubate

Fledging: 25 days; male and female lead their young to food

Migration: complete, to western states and Mexico

Food: insects

Compare: The Spotted Sandpiper (pg. 131) is found around water and lacks the 2 neck bands of the Killdeer. Semipalmated Plover (pg. 127) shares the brown back and white belly, but is smaller and has a single black necklace.

Stan's Notes: The only shorebird with two black neck bands. It is known for its broken wing impression, which draws intruders away from nest. Once clear of the nest, the Killdeer takes flight. Nests are only a slight depression in a gravel area, often very difficult to see. Young look like yellow cotton balls on stilts when first hatched, but quickly molt to appear similar to parents. Able to follow parents and peck for insects soon after birth. Is technically classified as a shorebird, but doesn't live at the shore. Often found in vacant fields or along railroads. Has a very distinctive "kill-deer" call.

male

in flight

juvenile

female

in flight
juvenile

MIGRATION
SUMMER

American Kestrel
Falco sparverius

Size: 10-12" (25-30 cm); up to 2-foot wingspan

Male: Rusty brown back and tail. A white breast with dark spots. Double black vertical lines on white face. Blue gray wings. Distinctive wide black band with a white edge on tip of rusty tail.

Female: similar to male, but slightly larger, has rusty brown wings and dark bands on tail

Juvenile: same as adult of the same sex

Nest: cavity; doesn't build a nest within; 1 brood per year

Eggs: 4-5; white with brown markings

Incubation: 29-31 days; male and female incubate

Fledging: 30-31 days; female and male feed young

Migration: complete, to western states

Food: insects, small mammals and birds, reptiles

Compare: Peregrine Falcon (pg. 291) is larger and has a dark "hood" and mustache mark. Look for 2 vertical black stripes on Kestrel's face.

Stan's Notes: A falcon that was once called Sparrow Hawk due to its small size. Could be called Grasshopper Hawk because it eats many grasshoppers. Can see ultraviolet light; this ability helps it locate mice and other small mammals by their urine, which glows bright yellow in ultraviolet light. Hovers near roads before diving for prey. Adapts quickly to a wooden nest box. Has pointed swept-back wings, seen in flight. Perches nearly upright. Unusual raptor in that males and females have quite different markings. Watch for them to pump their tails up and down after landing on perches.

male

female

Northern Flicker
Colaptes auratus

Size: 12" (30 cm)

Male: Brown and black woodpecker with a large white rump patch visible only when flying. Black necklace above a speckled chest. Gray head with a brown cap. Red mustache.

Female: same as male, but lacking a red mustache

Juvenile: same as adult of the same sex

Nest: cavity; female and male excavate; 1 brood per year

Eggs: 5-8; white without markings

Incubation: 11-14 days; female and male incubate

Fledging: 25-28 days; female and male feed young

Migration: complete, to western states

Food: insects, especially ants and beetles

Compare: The only woodpecker in Alaska that has a brown back. Hairy Woodpecker (pg. 31) is smaller and has a white stripe down its back. Look for the speckled breast and gray head of Northern Flicker to help identify.

Stan's Notes: This is the only woodpecker to regularly feed on the ground. Preferring ants and beetles, it produces an antacid saliva to neutralize the acidic defense of ants. Male usually selects a nest site, taking up to 12 days to excavate. Some people have had success attracting flickers to nest boxes stuffed with sawdust. During flight, flashes reddish orange under the wings and tail. Undulates deeply in flight while giving loud "wacka-wacka" calls.

Upland Sandpiper
Bartramia longicauda

Size: 12" (30 cm)

Male: Overall brown shorebird. Long yellow legs, a short, brown-tipped yellow bill and white belly. Appears to have a thin neck and small head in relationship to its body.

Female: same as male

Juvenile: similar to adult

Nest: ground; female and male construct; 1 brood per year

Eggs: 3-4; off-white with red markings

Incubation: 21-27 days; female and male incubate

Fledging: 30 31 days; female and male feed young

Migration: complete, to South America

Food: insects, seeds

Compare: Breeding Spotted Sandpiper (pg. 131) is smaller, has shorter legs, black spots on a white breast and is found in very different habitats. The Spotted Sandpiper is almost always near water while the Upland is in grassy meadows and prairies.

Stan's Notes: A shorebird of the dry grassland that is aptly named. Often seen standing on fence posts or other perches in a prairie or grassland habitat. Frequently found in prairies and grasslands that were burned, where foraging for food is easier. A true indicator of high-quality prairie habitat, this shorebird returns to a more watery habitat after breeding and just before migrating. Frequently holds its wings open over its back for several seconds just after landing. Formerly known as Upland Plover. Was hunted in the late 1800s.

breeding
male

winter
pg. 335

breeding
female

YEAR-ROUND

White-tailed Ptarmigan
Lagopus leucura

Size: 12½" (32 cm)

Male: Breeding (Apr-Jul) has speckled brown and black sides and a white belly. Red eyebrows (combs). Feathered legs and feet. Small dark bill. White-sided tail, seen in flight.

Female: dark brown with scattered white on sides, feathered legs and feet, small dark bill

Juvenile: similar to breeding female, white on wings

Nest: ground; female builds; 1 brood per year

Eggs: 4-8; tan with brown markings

Incubation: 22-24 days; female incubates

Fledging: 10-15 days; female shows young what to eat

Migration: non-migrator to partial; will move around in winter to find food

Food: leaf and flower buds, seeds, insects, berries

Compare: The breeding Rock Ptarmigan (pg. 155) is overall darker. Breeding Willow Ptarmigan (pg. 157) is rusty brown. Look for the white sides of tail to help identify.

Stan's Notes: Male displays swollen red combs when courting and alternates fast with slow strutting. Female builds a shallow nest in spring, usually under a shrub, and lines it with fine grass, lichens and feathers. She delays nesting until fully molted into her summer camouflage plumage. If threatened at the nest, female will perform a distraction display that includes hissing and clucking. Male leaves female shortly after eggs hatch. Species name *leucura* is Greek and means "white tail." Other ptarmigans have black-sided tails. Molts in late fall to white plumage and blends into the winter landscape.

breeding male

winter male pg. 337

breeding female

Rock Ptarmigan
Lagopus muta

YEAR-ROUND

Size: 14" (36 cm)

Male: Breeding (Apr-Jul) is overall brown, but can be gray to nearly black. Bright red eyebrows (combs). White belly and sides. Small dark bill. Feathered legs and feet. Black-sided tail, seen in flight.

Female: dark brown overall with white wing tips, feathered legs and feet, small dark bill

Juvenile: similar to breeding female, white outermost flight feathers

Nest: ground; female builds; 1 brood per year

Eggs: 6-9; tan with brown markings

Incubation: 21-24 days; female incubates

Fledging: 12-20 days; female shows young what to eat

Migration: non-migrator to partial; will move around in winter to find food

Food: leaf and flower buds, seeds, insects, berries

Compare: The breeding male White-tailed Ptarmigan (pg. 153) has black speckles on its sides. The breeding Willow Ptarmigan (pg. 157) is rusty brown. Look for black sides on the tail to identify the Rock Ptarmigan.

Stan's Notes: Male displays his bright red combs to female. Female builds a shallow ground nest, usually among rocks, and covers it with vegetation until her clutch is complete. Male leaves the female when she starts to incubate. The common name comes from its habitat on rocky tundra. Latin species name *muta* means "animal that can only mutter or has a weak call" and refers to its quiet call.

breeding
male

winter
pg. 339

breeding
female

YEAR-ROUND

Willow Ptarmigan
Lagopus lagopus

Size: 14" (36 cm)

Male: Breeding plumage (May-Jul) has a rusty red head, neck and upper breast. Brown back and top of wings. White lower breast and belly, often speckled with rusty red. Dark red eyebrows. Feathered legs and feet. Stout dark bill. Black edges on tail, seen in flight.

Female: light brown overall, feathered legs and feet, stout dark bill

Juvenile: similar to breeding female, white on wings

Nest: ground; female builds; 1 brood per year

Eggs: 5-14; blackish brown with cream markings

Incubation: 21-23 days; female incubates

Fledging: 10-14 days; female shows young what to eat

Migration: non-migrator to partial; will move around in winter to find food

Food: buds (mainly willow), seeds, insects

Compare: Breeding Rock Ptarmigan (pg. 155) and White-tailed Ptarmigan (pg. 153) lack the rusty red head, neck and upper breast.

Stan's Notes: "Ptarmigan" comes from a Gaelic word for this kind of bird, *tarmachan*. Common name comes from its favor for willow buds and leaves. In spring, female molts to a camouflage coloration that enables her to blend with landscape during incubation. Nests on open tundra. Lines its nest with leaves, grass and a few feathers. Unlike other ptarmigan species, male remains with female to raise young. However, the females without mates are just as successful rearing their young as the females with mates.

MIGRATION
SUMMER

Greater Yellowlegs
Tringa melanoleuca

Size: 14" (36 cm)

Male: Tall bird with a bulbous head and long thin bill, slightly upturned. Gray streaking on chest. White belly. Long yellow legs.

Female: same as male

Juvenile: same as adult

Nest: ground; female builds; 1 brood per year

Eggs: 3-4; off-white with brown markings

Incubation: 22-23 days; female and male incubate

Fledging: 18-20 days; male and female feed yo

Migration: complete, to California, Texas, Mexico and Central and South America

Food: small fish, aquatic insects

Compare: Nearly identical to the Lesser Yellowlegs (pg. 141), only larger and has an upturned, longer bill. Whimbrel (pg. 183) is larger and lacks the yellow legs.

Stan's Notes: Common shorebird seen in southern parts of Alaska. Can be identified by the slightly upturned bill and long yellow legs. Often seen resting on one leg. Its long legs carry it through deep water. Feeds by rushing forward through the water, plowing its bill or swinging it from side to side, catching small fish and insects. A skittish bird that is quick to give an alarm call, causing flocks to take flight. Quite often moves into water prior to taking flight. Has a variety of "flight" notes that it gives when taking off. Nests on the ground near water. Migrates earlier than Lesser Yellowlegs in spring and later in fall.

male pg. 45

female

Bufflehead
Bucephala albeola

Size: 13-15" (33-38 cm)

Female: Brownish gray duck with dark brown head. White patch on cheek, just behind eyes.

Male: striking black and white duck with a head that shines green purple in sunlight, large white bonnet-like patch on back of head

Juvenile: similar to female

Nest: cavity; female lines old woodpecker cavity; 1 brood per year

Eggs: 8-10; ivory to olive without markings

Incubation: 29-31 days; female incubates

Fledging: 50-55 days; female leads young to food

Migration: complete, to southern coastal Alaska, western states, Mexico and Central America

Food: aquatic insects

Compare: Smaller than female Lesser Scaup (pg. 171), which has a white patch at the base of bill unlike the female Bufflehead's white patch on the cheek.

Stan's Notes: Common diving duck that travels with other ducks. Found on rivers and lakes. Nests in old woodpecker cavities. Has been known to use a burrow in an earthen bank when tree cavities are scarce. Will use a nest box. Uses only down feathers to line the nest cavity. Unlike other ducks, young remain in the nest for up to two days before venturing out with their mother. Female is very territorial and remains with the same mate for many years.

YEAR-ROUND
SUMMER

Green-winged Teal
Anas crecca

Size: 15" (38 cm)

Male: A chestnut head with a dark green patch in back of eyes extending down to nape and outlined in white. Gray body. Butter yellow tail. Green patch on wings (speculum), seen in flight.

Female: light brown in color with black spots, green speculum, small black bill

Juvenile: same as female

Nest: ground; female builds; 1 brood per year

Eggs: 8-10; creamy white without markings

Incubation: 21-23 days; female incubates

Fledging: 32-34 days; female teaches young to feed

Migration: complete to non-migrator in Alaska

Food: aquatic plants and insects

Compare: The female Blue-winged Teal (pg. 165) is similar in size, but has slight white at base of bill. Look for a dark green patch on each side of a chestnut head to identify the male Green-winged Teal.

Stan's Notes: One of the smallest dabbling ducks, it tips forward in the water to feed off the bottom of shallow ponds. This behavior makes it vulnerable to ingesting spent lead shot, which can cause death. It walks well on land and also feeds in fields and woodlands. Known for its fast and agile flight, groups spin and wheel through the air in tight formation. Green speculum most obvious in flight.

MIGRATION
SUMMER

Blue-winged Teal
Anas discors

Size: 15-16" (38-40 cm)

Male: Small, plain-looking brown duck speckled with black. A gray head with a large white crescent-shaped mark at base of bill. Black tail with small white patch. Blue wing patch (speculum), usually seen only in flight.

Female: duller than male, lacks white patch on tail, has only slight white at base of bill

Juvenile: same as female

Nest: ground; female builds; 1 brood per year

Eggs: 8-11; creamy white

Incubation: 23-27 days; female incubates

Fledging: 35-44 days; female feeds young

Migration: complete, to western states and Mexico

Food: aquatic plants, seeds, aquatic insects

Compare: Male Blue-winged Teal has a distinct white marking on each side of face. The female Green-winged Teal (pg. 163) lacks white at base of bill. The female Blue-winged Teal is smaller than female Mallard (pg. 205).

Stan's Notes: One of the smallest ducks in North America. Nests some distance from water. Female performs a distraction display to protect nest and young. Male leaves female near end of incubation. Planting crops and cultivating to pond edges have caused a decline in population. Widespread nesting in North America, breeding as far north as central Alaska. One of the most common and longest distance migrating ducks.

Short-eared Owl
Asio flammeus

YEAR-ROUND
SUMMER

Size: 15½" (39 cm); up to 3-foot wingspan

Male: Overall brown to gray with a large round head and light face. Heavy streaking on the chest with lighter belly. Spotted back. Black "wrist" mark. Very short, tiny ear tufts, often not noticeable. Bright yellow eyes and dark eye patches.

Female: same as male, but overall darker

Juvenile: similar to adults, light gray with a dark face

Nest: platform, on the ground; takes over a crow, squirrel or hawk nest; 1 brood per year

Eggs: 4-6; white without markings

Incubation: 26-28 days; female incubates

Fledging: 23-26 days; male and female feed young

Migration: complete to partial migrator

Food: small mammals, birds

Compare: Northern Hawk Owl (pg. 169) is similar in size, but it has a much smaller head and longer tail. Stiff wing beats and erratic flight make the Short-eared Owl easy to identify.

Stan's Notes: Seen throughout Alaska in summer and year-round along the southeastern coast. Hunts over open fields, often floating on its long wings just before dropping onto prey. Flies with long, slow wing beats. Male calls from high above the nest site, soaring, occasionally swooping and clapping wings together beneath its body. Perches on the ground. Distinctive black "wrist" mark under wings and a bold tan patch near upper end of wings, seen in flight.

in flight

Northern Hawk Owl
Surnia ulula

Size: 16" (40 cm); up to 2½-foot wingspan

Male: Overall brown to gray. Many fine rusty bars horizontally from breast to tail. White face with a black frame. Dark and light speckled forehead. Broad, flat top of head and bright yellow eyes. Long pointed tail. Yellow bill.

Female: same as male, only slightly larger

Juvenile: light gray with a dark face, yellow eyes

Nest: cavity or platform; takes over crow or hawk nest, sometimes on top of stump, does not add any nesting material; 1 brood per year

Eggs: 5-7; white without markings

Incubation: 25-30 days; female incubates

Fledging: 25-35 days; male and female feed young

Migration: non-migrator to irruptive; moves around Alaska in winter to find food

Food: mice, other small mammals, birds, insects

Compare: Similar size as Short-eared Owl (pg. 167), but has a smaller head and longer tail. Look for Hawk Owl's powerful hawk-like flight and swooping approach before landing.

Stan's Notes: A uniquely shaped owl that flies like a hawk (hence its common name) with fast, stiff wing beats. Flies close to ground, swooping up to a perch on a pole or tree. Can hover. Often covers feet while perching. Frequently hunts during the day. Caches extra mice and voles in the forks of trees. Will use a nest box on a tree. Usually unafraid of people.

male pg. 51

female

SUMMER

Lesser Scaup
Aythya affinis

Size: 16-17" (40-43 cm)

Female: Overall brown duck with dull white patch at base of light gray bill. Yellow eyes.

Male: white and gray, the chest and head appear nearly black but head appears purple with green highlights in direct sun, yellow eyes

Juvenile: same as female

Nest: ground; female builds; 1 brood per year

Eggs: 8-14; olive buff without markings

Incubation: 22-28 days; female incubates

Fledging: 45-50 days; female teaches young to feed

Migration: complete, to western states and Mexico

Food: aquatic plants and insects

Compare: Nearly identical to the female Greater Scaup (pg. 187), which has a more rounded head and a bold white patch at the base of bill. The male Blue-winged Teal (pg. 165) has a large crescent-shaped white mark at base of bill. The female Canvasback (pg. 203) has a sloping forehead and long dark bill.

Stan's Notes: A common diving duck. Often seen in large flocks on lakes, ponds and sewage lagoons. Completely submerges itself to feed on the bottom of lakes (unlike dabbling ducks, which only tip forward to reach the bottom). Note the bold white stripe under the wings when in flight. Male leaves female when she starts to incubate the eggs. Quantity of eggs (clutch size) increases with the age of the female. An interesting baby-sitting arrangement in which groups of young (crèches) are tended by 1-3 adult females.

male pg. 53

female

Harlequin Duck
Histrionicus histrionicus

YEAR-ROUND
SUMMER

Size: 17" (43 cm)

Female: Overall brown duck with a white patch on the sides of head and near the base of bill. Short bill. Long pointed tail.

Male: black and white duck with rusty red sides and top of head, highest part of head above eyes, small light-colored bill, long pointed tail; winter is overall brown with a white patch at base of bill and sides of head, faint white marks at shoulders and base of tail

Juvenile: similar to female

Nest: ground; female builds; 1 brood per year

Eggs: 6-8; pale white without markings

Incubation: 28-31 days; female incubates

Fledging: 60-70 days; female leads young to food

Migration: partial to non-migrator, to southern coastal Alaska

Food: aquatic insects, crustaceans, mollusks

Compare: Same size as the female Long-tailed Duck (pg. 55), which has white around the eyes and a large white rump.

Stan's Notes: A small duck that rides low in water. Found in fast-running rivers and streams, which presumably have a richer food supply than slow-moving water. Frequently walks in shallow water, foraging for food on the bottom among the rocks. Uses wings and feet to propel itself underwater unlike other diving ducks, which just use their feet. Female does not breed until 2 years of age. Male leaves female after she starts to incubate.

male

female

YEAR-ROUND

Spruce Grouse
Falcipennis canadensis

Size: 17" (43 cm); up to 2-foot wingspan

Male: Plump grouse, brown to almost black, with white speckles on the chest and belly. Short neck, red eyebrows (combs) and short dark tail with a chestnut tip.

Female: overall brown grouse with small black and white barring on the chest, dark brown tail with a chestnut tip

Juvenile: similar to female

Nest: ground; female builds; 1 brood per year

Eggs: 4-7; tan with brown markings

Incubation: 17-24 days; female incubates

Fledging: 8-10 days; male and female feed young

Migration: non-migrator; moves around to find food

Food: coniferous needles, insects, seeds, berries

Compare: Ruffed Grouse (pg. 179) is lighter brown and has a tuft of feathers on the head. The Sharp-tailed Grouse (pg. 177) has yellow eyebrows and a narrow, pointed white tail.

Stan's Notes: Well known for being semi-tame and approachable. In winter it is often seen in groups along roads, where snow isn't as deep and small rocks can be eaten to aid in digestion. Prefers open coniferous forests. Eats mainly spruce needles, hence its common name. Roosts in trees. Displaying male fans tail, leans forward and droops wings while quickly flapping wings in a short flight. Female is territorial against other females. The cryptic coloring of the female allows her to blend in with the surroundings. Often freezes when danger approaches, hence its other common name, Fool Hen.

YEAR-ROUND

Sharp-tailed Grouse
Tympanuchus phasianellus

Size: 16-18" (40-45 cm); up to 2-foot wingspan

Male: Overall brown grouse with white and dark brown-to-black marks. Paler below. Yellow eyebrows (combs). Pale purple throat sacs. Small crest. A narrow, pointed white tail.

Female: similar to non-displaying male

Juvenile: similar to female

Nest: ground; female builds; 1 brood per year

Eggs: 5-15; light brown with brown markings

Incubation: 21-24 days; female incubates

Fledging: 7-10 days; female leads young to food

Migration: non-migrator; moves around to find food

Food: seeds, nuts, insects, berries, leaves

Compare: Similar size as the Ruffed Grouse (pg. 179), which has a squared dark tail. Male Spruce Grouse (pg. 175) has red eyebrows and is dark brown to nearly black. Look for the Sharp-tailed's narrow, pointed white tail.

Stan's Notes: An upland game species named for its pointed tail. Males gather in groups of up to 20 birds in an area called a lek to dance and display. Leks are often used for many years. Displaying males will bow forward, droop wings at their sides and point tails straight up in the air. Appearing like wind-up toys, they stamp their feet quickly and produce a loud rattling noise that resonates from the throat sac, which is inflated with air. Females will choose the best dancers, which tend to be the older, more experienced males. Often these males are in the center of the group.

drumming

Ruffed Grouse
Bonasa umbellus

Size: 16-19" (40-48 cm); up to 2-foot wingspan

Male: Brown chicken-like bird with long squared tail. Wide black band near tip of tail. Is able to fan tail like a turkey. Tuft of feathers on the head stands like a crown. Black ruffs on sides of neck.

Female: same as male, but less obvious neck ruffs

Juvenile: same as female

Nest: ground; female builds; 1 brood per year

Eggs: 9-12; tan with light brown markings

Incubation: 23-24 days; female incubates

Fledging: 10-12 days; female leads young to food

Migration: non-migrator; moves around to find food

Food: seeds, insects, fruit, leaf buds

Compare: Slightly larger and lighter brown than the Spruce Grouse (pg. 175), which has a darker tail. Look for feathered tuft on head and black neck ruffs.

Stan's Notes: A common bird of deep woods. Often seen in aspen or other trees, feeding on leaf buds. In the more northern climates, grows bristles on its feet during the winter to serve as snowshoes. When there is enough snow, it will dive into a snowbank to roost at night. In spring, male raises its crest (tuft), fans tail feathers, and stands on logs and drums with wings to attract females. Drumming sound comes from cupped wings moving the air, not pounding on its chest or a log. Female will perform distraction display to protect young. Two color morphs, red and gray, most apparent in the tail. Black ruffs around the neck gave rise to its common name.

Bristle-thighed Curlew
Numenius tahitiensis

Size: 17½"(44 cm)

Male: Brown shorebird with a long down-curved bill, dark cap and dark brown line through the eyes. Rusty red wing linings. Pale rump. Gray legs and feet.

Female: same as male

Juvenile: similar to adult

Nest: ground; female and male construct; 1 brood per year

Eggs: 3-5; pale olive green with brown markings

Incubation: 27-30 days; female and male incubate

Fledging: 32-42 days; female and male feed young

Migration: complete, to Pacific islands

Food: insects, fruit, seeds

Compare: Nearly identical to the Whimbrel (pg. 183), which has brown-to-gray wing linings and a brown rump.

Stan's Notes: A bird of the mountain tundra. Nests in dry exposed ridges made from lichens, with little or no lining. Seen wintering on Pacific islands but it was unknown where nesting grounds were located until the 1940s, when it was discovered nesting on high mountains in northwestern Alaska. Has a relatively short migration compared with other shorebirds. Unlike the widespread range of the Whimbrel, the Bristle-thighed has a limited range in Alaska.

Whimbrel
Numenius phaeopus

Size: 18" (45 cm)

Male: Heavily streaked bird, light brown to gray. A long down-curved bill and multiple dark brown stripes on the crown. Brown-to-gray wing linings. Dark line through eyes. Legs are light gray to blue.

Female: same as male

Juvenile: similar to adult

Nest: ground; female and male construct; 1 brood per year

Eggs: 3-4; olive green with dark markings

Incubation: 27-28 days; male and female incubate

Fledging: 35-42 days; female and male feed young

Migration: complete, to coastal California and Mexico

Food: insects, snails, worms, leeches, berries

Compare: Bristle-thighed Curlew (pg. 181) has rusty red wing linings and rump. The Greater Yellowlegs (pg. 159) has yellow legs. Short-billed Dowitcher (pg. 143) has a straight bill. The breeding Red Knot (pg. 327) has a reddish belly and a much shorter bill.

Stan's Notes: A breeding bird and seen during migration in Alaska. Easy to identify by its very long down-curved bill and brown stripes on head. Uses its bill to probe deep into sand and mud for insects. Unlike the other shorebirds, berries are an important food source in summer. Very vocal, giving single note whistles. Doesn't breed until age 3. Has a long-term pair bond. Adults leave breeding grounds up to two weeks before the young leave.

breeding pg. 63

winter

Red-necked Grebe
Podiceps grisegena

Size: 18" (45 cm)

Male: Winter (Sep-Mar) is overall brown with a large, slightly darker head and lighter neck. Long, thin yellow bill.

Female: same as male

Juvenile: similar to winter adult

Nest: floating platform; female and male build; 1 brood per year

Eggs: 3-6; white without markings

Incubation: 21-23 days; female and male incubate

Fledging: 50-70 days; female and male feed young

Migration: complete to non-migrator in Alaska

Food: aquatic insects, small fish

Compare: The winter Common Murre (pg. 57) and winter Thick-billed Murre (pg. 59) have a brownish black back and white lower body.

Stan's Notes: One of seven grebe species in North America. Like the other grebes, it has a tiny tail that is usually hidden in its fluffy feathers at the base of tail (coverts). It has lobed toes unlike ducks, which have webbed feet. Found in small ponds and shallow lakes lined with reeds and sedges. Forages for food by diving for aquatic insects, often remaining underwater for up to a minute. Doesn't fly much once at nesting grounds. Builds a floating nest with plants and anchors it to one spot. Floating keeps nest from submerging when water rises during spring snowmelt. Young hatch one day at a time (asynchronously). Parents feed the young tiny feathers. This presumably helps protect the stomach lining from bones in fish, its main diet. Populations have decreased over the past 30 years.

male pg. 61

female

MIGRATION
SUMMER

Greater Scaup
Aythya marila

Size: 18" (45 cm)

Female: An overall brown duck with a darker head and a bold white patch at the base of bill. Might show a white patch behind each eye. Rounded top of head.

Male: mostly black and white, black head shines green in direct sunlight, bright white sides and a gray back, light blue bill with a black tip, rounded head

Juvenile: same as female

Nest: ground; female builds; 1 brood per year

Eggs: 7-10; greenish olive without markings

Incubation: 24-28 days; female incubates

Fledging: 45-50 days; female teaches young to feed

Migration: complete, to western coastal U.S., Mexico

Food: aquatic plants and insects

Compare: The female Lesser Scaup (pg. 171) is very similar, but has a more pointed head and lacks the bold white patch at base of bill. Female Canvasback (pg. 203) is larger and has a sloping forehead and long dark bill.

Stan's Notes: Common summer resident and migrant, breeding in the southern two-thirds of Alaska. More common than the Lesser Scaup, but before 1920, the Lesser Scaup was more common. Most abundant on large saltwater bays.

male pg. 289

female

Gadwall
Anas strepera

Size: 19" (48 cm)

Female: Mottled brown with a pronounced color change from dark brown body to light brown neck and head. Wing linings are bright white, seen in flight. Small white wing patch, seen when swimming. Gray bill with orange sides.

Male: plump gray duck with a brown head and distinctive black rump, white belly, bright white wing linings, small white wing patch, chestnut-tinged wings, gray bill

Juvenile: similar to female

Nest: ground; female lines the nest with fine grass and down feathers plucked from her chest; 1 brood per year

Eggs: 8-11; white without markings

Incubation: 24-27 days; female incubates

Fledging: 48-56 days; young feed themselves

Migration: complete to non-migrator in Alaska

Food: aquatic insects

Compare: The female Gadwall is very similar to female Mallard (pg. 205). Look for Gadwall's white wing patch and gray bill with orange sides.

Stan's Notes: A duck of shallow marshes. Consumes mostly plant material, dunking its head in water to feed rather than tipping forward, like other dabbling ducks. Walks well on land; feeds in fields and woodlands. Nests within 300 feet (100 m) of water. Often in pairs with other duck species. Establishes pair bond during winter.

American Wigeon
Anas americana

YEAR-ROUND
MIGRATION
SUMMER

Size: 19" (48 cm)

Male: A brown duck with a rounded head, a long pointed tail and short, black-tipped grayish bill. Obvious white cap. Deep green patch starting behind eyes, streaking down neck. White belly and wing linings, seen in flight. Non-breeding lacks white cap, green patch.

Female: light brown with a pale gray head, a short, black-tipped grayish bill, green wing patch (speculum), dark eye spot, white belly and wing linings, seen in flight

Juvenile: similar to female

Nest: ground; female builds; 1 brood per year

Eggs: 7-12; white without markings

Incubation: 23-25 days; female incubates

Fledging: 37-48 days; female teaches young to feed

Migration: complete, to western states and Mexico

Food: aquatic plants, seeds

Compare: Male American Wigeon is easily identified by the white cap and black-tipped grayish bill. Look for a black-tipped grayish bill and green wing patch to help identify the female American Wigeon.

Stan's Notes: Often in small flocks or with other ducks. Prefers shallow lakes. Male stays with female the first week of incubation only. Female raises young. If threatened, female feigns injury while young run and hide. Conceals upland nest in tall vegetation within 50-250 yards (46-228 m) of water.

male pg. 65

female

YEAR-ROUND
SUMMER
WINTER

Barrow's Goldeneye
Bucephala islandica

Size: 18-20" (45-50 cm)

Female: A large dark brown head. Gray body. Bright golden eyes. Small mostly yellow bill. White collar around neck, often hidden.

Male: black and white duck with large puffy head, head appears deep green in bright sunlight, a low, flat top of head, bright golden eyes, large crescent-shaped white mark in front of each eye, small dark bill

Juvenile: same as female, but has a dark bill

Nest: cavity; female lines old woodpecker cavity; 1 brood per year

Eggs: 9-11; green to olive without markings

Incubation: 32-34 days; female incubates

Fledging: 55-60 days; female leads young to food

Migration: partial to non-migrator, to southern coastal Alaska and western coastal states

Food: aquatic insects and plants, mollusks

Compare: Nearly identical to the female Common Goldeneye (pg. 195), which has a yellow-tipped dark bill.

Stan's Notes: Nests in cavities near ponds and lakes. Will also use a nest box. Female often returns to the same nest location for many years. Female may mate with the same male from year to year. Male leaves female once she starts incubating. Young remain in the nest 24-36 hours before fledging. Often swims out to open water when threatened instead of flying away. Will hybridize with the closely related Common Goldeneye, producing a bird with a maroon head.

female

male pg. 67

SUMMER
WINTER

Common Goldeneye
Bucephala clangula

Size: 18½-20" (47-50 cm)

Female: A brown and gray duck with a large dark brown head and gray body. White collar. Bright golden eyes. Yellow-tipped dark bill.

Male: mostly white duck with a black back and a large, puffy green head, large white spot in front of each bright golden eye, dark bill

Juvenile: same as female, but has a dark bill

Nest: cavity; female lines old woodpecker cavity; 1 brood per year

Eggs: 8-10; light green without markings

Incubation: 28-32 days; female incubates

Fledging: 56-59 days; female leads young to food

Migration: complete, to southern coastal Alaska, western states and Mexico

Food: aquatic plants, insects, fish, mollusks

Compare: The female Barrow's Goldeneye (pg. 193) is nearly identical, but has a yellow bill. The female Lesser Scaup (pg. 171) is similar, but smaller. Look for the female Common Goldeneye's large dark brown head and white collar.

Stan's Notes: Known for its loud whistling, produced by its wings in flight. In late winter and early spring, male often attracts female through elaborate displays, throwing its head backward while it utters a single raspy note. Female will lay eggs in other goldeneye nests, which results in some mothers incubating up to 30 eggs. Received the common name from its obvious bright golden eyes.

male pg. 13

female

MIGRATION
SUMMER
WINTER

Black Scoter
Melanitta nigra

Size: 19¼" (49 cm)

Female: An all-brown duck with a dark crown, pale white cheeks and thin dark bill.

Male: all-black duck with a large yellow knob at the base of bill and a narrow pointed tail

Juvenile: similar to female

Nest: ground; female builds; 1 brood per year

Eggs: 6-8; light pink to buff without markings

Incubation: 30-31 days; female incubates

Fledging: 45-50 days; female feeds young

Migration: complete, to southern coastal Alaska, western coastal U.S. and Mexico

Food: mollusks, crustaceans, aquatic plants, seeds

Compare: Smaller than female White-winged Scoter (pg. 201), which has a white patch in front of each eye and a larger bill. Slightly smaller than female Surf Scoter (pg. 199), which has a vertical white patch at the base of bill and a white mark on the nape.

Stan's Notes: The least common of scoters, although once known as the Common Scoter. Often in mixed flocks numbering in the hundreds along the coast during migration and winter. Usually will feed in seawater 20-40 feet (6-12 m) deep, just outside the breaker zone. Nests on the tundra close to freshwater lakes and ponds, returning to sea after breeding season for the rest of the summer and winter. Female doesn't breed until her third summer. Male will leave female shortly after she starts to incubate. Broods sometimes gather in groups called crèches and are tended by 1-3 older females.

male pg. 69

female

Surf Scoter
Melanitta perspicillata

MIGRATION
SUMMER
WINTER

Size: 20" (50 cm)

Female: Brown duck with a dark crown and white mark on nape. Vertical white patch at the base of a large dark bill. Bright white eyes.

Male: black with a white patch on forehead and nape, multicolored bill with a white base, black spot and orange tip, bright white eyes

Juvenile: similar to female

Nest: ground; female builds; 1 brood per year

Eggs: 5-8; light pink to buff without markings

Incubation: 30-31 days; female incubates

Fledging: 45-50 days; female feeds young

Migration: complete, to southern coastal Alaska, western coastal U.S. and Mexico

Food: mollusks, crustaceans, aquatic insects

Compare: Slightly larger than the female Black Scoter (pg. 197), which has white cheeks and a much smaller bill. Slightly smaller than the female White-winged Scoter (pg. 201), which lacks the vertical white patch at the base of its bill and white mark on nape.

Stan's Notes: Dives or scoots through breaking surf. However, the common name "Scoter" may refer to the sooty black color of its plumage. Dives down to 40 feet (12 m) in seawater, foraging for mussels and crustaceans. Fish eggs make up 90 percent of its diet during spring and early summer. Nests on the tundra in Alaska near freshwater lakes and ponds. Spends the winter at sea, rarely returning to shore. Sometimes in mixed flocks with other scoters.

male pg. 15

female

White-winged Scoter
Melanitta fusca

MIGRATION
SUMMER
WINTER

Size: 20½" (52 cm)

Female: Brown duck with a dark crown. Large dull white patch just behind the eyes and at the base of a large dark bill.

Male: black duck with a white patch underneath each eye, large bicolored yellow and orange bill, bright white eyes

Juvenile: similar to female

Nest: ground; female builds; 1 brood per year

Eggs: 5-10; light pink to buff without markings

Incubation: 28-31 days; female incubates

Fledging: 50-60 days; female feeds young

Migration: complete, to southern coastal Alaska, western coastal U.S. and Mexico

Food: mollusks, crustaceans, aquatic insects and plants

Compare: Larger than female Black Scoter (pg. 197), which has white cheeks and a smaller bill. Slightly larger than the female Surf Scoter (pg. 199), which has a vertical white patch at the base of bill and white mark on nape.

Stan's Notes: Nests on the tundra in Alaska near freshwater lakes and ponds. Spends the winter at sea, rarely returning to shore. Sometimes in mixed flocks with other scoters. The genus name *Melanitta* from the Greek *melas* for "black" and *netta* for "duck" describes the bird well. The common name was first used in the *Collective Catalogue of Birds* (1674), but its origins are unknown.

male pg. 329

female

SUMMER

Canvasback
Aythya valisineria

Size: 20½" (52 cm)

Female: Brown head, neck and chest with light gray-to-brown sides. Long sloping forehead that transitions into a long dark bill.

Male: deep red head and neck, sloping forehead, long black bill, gray and white sides and back, black chest and tail

Juvenile: similar to female

Nest: ground; female builds; 1 brood per year

Eggs: 7-9; pale white to gray without markings

Incubation: 24-29 days; female incubates

Fledging: 56-67 days; female leads young to food

Migration: complete, to western coastal states, Mexico

Food: aquatic insects, small clams

Compare: Female Greater Scaup (pg. 187) and female Lesser Scaup (pg. 171) are smaller, have a white marking at the base of their bills and lack the sloping forehead and long dark bill of the female Canvasback.

Stan's Notes: A large inland duck of freshwater lakes, rivers and ponds. Populations declined dramatically in the 1960-80s due to marsh drainage for agriculture. Females return to their birthplace (philopatric) while males disperse to new areas. Will mate during migration or on the breeding grounds. A courting male gives a soft cooing call when displaying and during aerial chases. Male leaves the female after incubation starts. Female takes a new mate every year. Female feeds very little during incubation and will lose up to 70 percent of fat reserves during that time.

male pg. 309

female

Mallard
Anas platyrhynchos

Size: 20½" (52 cm)

Female: Brown duck with an orange and black bill and blue and white wing mark (speculum).

Male: large, bulbous green head, white necklace, rust brown or chestnut chest, combination of gray and white on the sides, yellow bill, orange legs and feet

Juvenile: same as female, but with a yellow bill

Nest: ground; female builds; 1 brood per year

Eggs: 7-10; greenish to whitish, unmarked

Incubation: 26-30 days; female incubates

Fledging: 42-52 days; female leads young to food

Migration: complete to non-migrator in parts of Alaska

Food: seeds, plants, aquatic insects; will come to ground feeders offering corn

Compare: Female Northern Pintail (pg. 207) is similar to the female Mallard, but has a gray bill. Female Northern Shoveler (pg. 173) is the same size, but has a large spoon-shaped bill.

Stan's Notes: A familiar duck of lakes and ponds, it's considered a type of dabbling duck, tipping forward in shallow water to feed on aquatic plants on the bottom. The name "Mallard" comes from the Latin *masculus*, meaning "male," referring to the habit of males not taking part in raising ducklings. Both female and male have white tails and white underwings. Black central tail feathers of male curl upward. Will return to place of birth.

SUMMER

Northern Pintail
Anas acuta

Size: 20½" (52 cm), female
25" (63 cm), male

Male: A slender, elegant duck with a brown head, white neck, gray body and extremely long, narrow black tail. Gray bill. Non-breeding has a pale brown head that lacks the clear demarcation between the brown head and white neck. Lacks long tail feathers.

Female: mottled brown body with a paler head and neck, long tail, gray bill

Juvenile: similar to female

Nest: ground; female builds; 1 brood per year

Eggs: 6-9; olive green without markings

Incubation: 22-25 days; female incubates

Fledging: 36-50 days; female teaches young to feed

Migration: complete, to western coastal states, Mexico

Food: aquatic plants and insects, seeds

Compare: The male Northern Pintail has a distinctive brown head and white neck. Look for the unique long tail feathers. The female Pintail is similar to female Mallard (pg. 205), but Mallard has an orange bill with black spots.

Stan's Notes: A common dabbling duck of marshes in the state. About 90 percent of its diet is aquatic plants, except when females feed heavily on aquatic insects prior to nesting, presumably to gain extra nutrients for egg production. Male holds tail upright from the water's surface. No other North American duck has such a long tail.

male pg. 311

female

SUMMER

Northern Shoveler
Anas clypeata

Size: 20½" (52 cm)

Female: Medium-sized brown duck speckled with black. Blue wing patch. An extraordinarily large spoon-shaped bill, almost always held pointed toward the water.

Male: iridescent green head, rusty sides and white breast, spoon-shaped bill

Juvenile: same as female

Nest: ground; female builds; 1 brood per year

Eggs: 9-12; olive without markings

Incubation: 22-25 days; female incubates

Fledging: 30-60 days; female leads young to food

Migration: complete, to southwestern states, Mexico

Food: aquatic insects, plants

Compare: Similar color as female Mallard (pg. 205), but Mallard lacks the Northern Shoveler's large bill. Look for Shoveler's spoon-shaped bill to help identify.

Stan's Notes: One of several species of shoveler, so called because of the peculiar shape of its bill. The first part of the common name was given because this is the only species of these ducks in North America. Found in small flocks of 5-10 birds, swimming low in water with its large bill pointed toward the water, as if it's too heavy to lift. Feeds mainly by filtering tiny aquatic insects and plants from the water's surface with its bill.

male
pg. 293

female

soaring

juvenile

soaring
juvenile

SUMMER

Northern Harrier
Circus cyaneus

Size: 18½-22½" (47-57 cm); up to 3½-ft. wingspan

Female: A slim, low-flying hawk. Dark brown back with brown-streaked breast and belly. Large white rump patch and narrow black bands across tail. Black wing tips. Yellow eyes.

Male: silver gray with large white rump patch and white belly, faint narrow bands across tail, black wing tips, yellow eyes

Juvenile: similar to female, with an orange breast

Nest: platform, often on ground; female and male build; 1 brood per year

Eggs: 4-8; bluish white without markings

Incubation: 31-32 days; female incubates

Fledging: 30-35 days; male and female feed young

Migration: complete, to western states and Mexico

Food: mice, snakes, insects, small birds

Compare: Slimmer than Red-tailed Hawk (pg. 213). Look for black tail bands, white rump patch and characteristic flight to help identify.

Stan's Notes: One of the easiest hawks to identify. Harriers glide just above ground, following contours of the land while searching for prey. Holds its wings just above the horizontal position, tilting back and forth in the wind. Formerly called Marsh Hawk due to its habit of hunting over marshes. Feeds on the ground. Will perch on the ground to preen and rest. At any age, has a distinctive owl-like face disk.

MIGRATION
SUMMER

Red-tailed Hawk
Buteo jamaicensis

Size: 19-23" (48-58 cm); up to 4-foot wingspan

Male: A large hawk with a wide variety of coloring from brown to white. Usually a white breast and a distinctive brown belly band. Rust red tail, usually seen only from above. White underside of wing with a small dark patch. Harlan's is brown to nearly black with white streaks on the upper breast. Gray-to-white tail, sometimes with narrow dark bands.

Female: same as male, only slightly larger

Juvenile: similar to adults, lacking the red tail, has a speckled chest and light eyes; Harlan's has a brown and white checkered pattern

Nest: platform; male and female build; 1 brood per year

Eggs: 2-3; white without markings or sometimes marked with brown

Incubation: 30-35 days; female and male incubate

Fledging: 45-46 days; male and female feed young

Migration: complete, to western states and Mexico

Food: mice, birds, snakes, insects, mammals

Compare: Rough-legged Hawk (pg. 215) has large, dark "wrist" marks, seen in flight.

Stan's Notes: A hawk of open country and cities, seen perching on freeway light posts, fences and trees. Look for it circling, searching for prey. Builds large stick nests in large trees along roads. Develops a red tail the second year. Harlan's is seen in the southern half of Alaska. Dark and light morphs. Map reflects the combined range.

soaring

soaring
juvenile

juvenile

light
morph

soaring

soaring
juvenile

juvenile

dark
morph

MIGRATION
SUMMER

Rough-legged Hawk
Buteo lagopus

Size: 22" (56 cm); up to 4½-foot wingspan

Male: A hawk of several plumages. All plumages have a long tail with a dark band or bands. Relatively long wings. Small bill and feet. Distinctive dark "wrists" and belly. Light morph has a nearly pure white underside of wings and base of tail. Dark morph is nearly all brown with a light gray trailing edge of wings.

Female: same as male, only larger

Juvenile: same as adults

Nest: platform, on edge of cliff; female and male build; 1 brood per year

Eggs: 2-6; white without markings

Incubation: 28-31 days; female and male incubate

Fledging: 39-43 days; female and male feed young

Migration: complete, to the northern half of the U.S.

Food: small mammals, snakes, large insects

Compare: Red-tailed Hawk (pg. 213) has a belly band and lacks dark "wrist" marks. The Osprey (pg. 73) has similar dark "wrists," but lacks the dark belly of the Rough-legged Hawk.

Stan's Notes: Two color morphs, light and dark, light being more common. A common summer resident and migrant in Alaska. Map reflects the combined range. More numerous in some years than in others. Has much smaller, weaker feet than other birds of prey and must hunt smaller prey. Hunts from the air, usually hovering before diving for small rodents such as mice and voles.

YEAR-ROUND

Great Horned Owl
Bubo virginianus

Size: 21-25" (53-63 cm); up to 3½-foot wingspan

Male: Robust brown "horned" owl. Bright yellow eyes and V-shaped white throat resembling a necklace. Horizontal barring on the chest.

Female: same as male, only slightly larger

Juvenile: similar to adults, lacking ear tufts

Nest: no nest; takes over a crow or hawk nest or will use a partial cavity, broken-off tree or stump; 1 brood per year

Eggs: 2; white without markings

Incubation: 26-30 days; female incubates

Fledging: 30-35 days; male and female feed young

Migration: non-migrator

Food: mammals, birds (ducks), snakes, insects

Compare: Smaller than the Great Gray Owl (pg. 301), which lacks ear tufts. Look for bright yellow eyes and feathers on head that look like horns to help identify the Great Horned.

Stan's Notes: One of the earliest nesting birds in the state, laying eggs in January and February. Has excellent hearing; able to hear a mouse moving beneath a foot of snow. "Ears" are actually tufts of feathers (horns) and have nothing to do with hearing. Not able to turn its head all the way around. Wing feathers are ragged on ends, resulting in a silent flight. The eyelids close from the top down, like humans. Fearless, it is one of the few animals that will kill skunks and porcupines. Because of this, it is sometimes called Flying Tiger.

male pg. 313

female

YEAR-ROUND
SUMMER

Red-breasted Merganser
Mergus serrator

Size: 23" (58 cm)

Female: Overall brown-to-gray duck with a shaggy reddish head and crest. Long orange bill.

Male: shaggy green head and crest, a prominent white collar, rusty breast, black and white body, long orange bill

Juvenile: similar to female

Nest: ground; female builds; 1 brood per year

Eggs: 5-10; olive green without markings

Incubation: 29-30 days; female incubates

Fledging: 55-65 days; female feeds young

Migration: complete to non-migrator in Alaska

Food: fish, aquatic insects

Compare: Smaller than female Common Merganser (pg. 331), which has a rusty red head and larger orange bill.

Stan's Notes: Breeding resident in Alaska. The most widespread of summer mergansers, arriving in April and leaving in October. Most commonly seen along the southeastern Alaska coast, but can also be seen in large inland freshwater lakes. A very fast flier, clocked at up to 100 miles (161 km) per hour. Usually seen flying low across the water. Needs a long run for takeoff with wings flapping to get airborne. Serrated bill helps it catch slippery fish. Usually a silent duck. Male occasionally gives a soft, catlike meow. Female gives a harsh "krrr-croak." Does not breed before 2 years. Male abandons female just after eggs are laid. Females will often share nests. Young leave the nest within 24 hours of hatching, never to return.

male pg. 75

female

Common Eider
Somateria mollissima

YEAR-ROUND
SUMMER
WINTER

Size: 24" (60 cm)

Female: Overall brown duck with a large body. Long sloping forehead that leads into a large gray bill. White wing linings, seen in flight.

Male: black and white with a large body, short neck, black cap, dark eyes, forehead slopes into a large yellow bill, green wash to nape

Juvenile: similar to female

Nest: ground; female builds; 1 brood per year

Eggs: 3-6; pale green without markings

Incubation: 25-30 days; female incubates

Fledging: 65-75 days; female leads young to food

Migration: partial to non-migrator

Food: aquatic insects

Compare: The large size, unique shape and forehead sloping into a large yellow bill make this duck easy to identify.

Stan's Notes: This is our largest sea duck. Found along the Pacific and Atlantic coasts. The western Arctic variety has a yellow bill, while the eastern variety has a green bill. Nests in small colonies on tundra ponds and rocky shores, usually within 100 feet (30 m) of water. Often prefers to nest on small islands that lack mammalian populations, especially Arctic Foxes. Mates may stay together for several years, but the male will leave the female shortly after she begins to incubate. Mothers usually don't eat while incubating, but leave to feed, regaining lost body fat after the young fledge. Two or three groups of ducklings gathered together (crèches) are tended by 1-2 older females.

Greater White-fronted Goose
Anser albifrons

Size: 28" (71 cm); up to 4½-foot wingspan

Male: Grayish brown bird with a distinctive white band at base of bill. Irregular black barring on the breast and belly. Bill is light pink to orange. Orange legs and feet. White rump and undertail.

Female: same as male

Juvenile: lighter color than adult and has yellowish legs, feet and bill

Nest: ground; female builds; 1 brood per year

Eggs: 4-7; creamy white without markings

Incubation: 23-25 days; female incubates

Fledging: 40-45 days; male and female teach young to feed

Migration: complete, to western coastal states, Mexico

Food: aquatic plants and insects

Compare: Similar size as the Snow Goose (pg. 353). White morph Snow Goose is all white with black wing tips and a large, bright pink bill. Blue morph Snow Goose often has a white head and dark gray body. Brant (pg. 77) has a dark head, neck and white necklace.

Stan's Notes: Summer resident in parts of Alaska and seen during migration. Hybridizes with Snow Geese and Canada Geese; often seen with them in mixed flocks or flying high up in large wedge shapes. Learns migratory route from parents and older members of flock. Does not breed until 3 years of age. Often called Speckled-bellied by hunters due to the irregular marking on the belly.

Golden Eagle
Aquila chrysaetos

Size: 30-40" (76-102 cm); up to 7-foot wingspan

Male: Uniform dark brown with a golden yellow head and nape of neck. Yellow around base of bill. Yellow feet.

Female: same as male

Juvenile: similar to adult, with white "wrist" patches and a white base of tail

Nest: platform, on a cliff; female and male build; 1 brood per year

Eggs: 2; white with brown markings

Incubation: 43-45 days; female and male incubate

Fledging: 66-75 days; female and male feed young

Migration: complete, to western states and Mexico

Food: mammals, birds, reptiles, insects

Compare: Similar to the adult Bald Eagle (pg. 81), but lacks the white head and tail. The juvenile Golden Eagle, a large dark bird with white markings, is often confused with juvenile Bald Eagle.

Stan's Notes: Large and powerful bird of prey that has no trouble taking larger prey such as jackrabbits. Hunts by perching or soaring and watching for movement. Inhabits mountainous terrain, requiring large territories to provide large supply of food. Thought to mate for life, renewing pair bond late in winter with spectacular high-flying courtship displays. Usually nests on cliff faces, rarely in trees. Uses well-established nest that has been used for generations. Not uncommon for it to add things to nest such as antlers, bones and barbed wire.

Golden-crowned Kinglet
Regulus satrapa

Size: 4" (10 cm)

Male: Tiny, plump green-to-gray bird. Distinctive yellow and orange patch with black border on the crown. A white eyebrow mark. Two white wing bars.

Female: same as male, but has a yellow crown with a black border, lacks any orange

Juvenile: same as adults, but lacks gold on crown

Nest: pendulous; female builds; 1-2 broods a year

Eggs: 5-9; white or creamy with brown markings

Incubation: 14-15 days; female incubates

Fledging: 14-19 days; female and male feed young

Migration: non-migrator in Alaska

Food: insects, fruit, tree sap

Compare: Similar to Ruby-crowned Kinglet (pg. 229), but Golden-crowned has an obvious crown. Arctic Warbler (pg. 231) is larger and lacks the black and yellowish crown.

Stan's Notes: Once considered a rare breeding bird in the state, it is now seen in parts of southern Alaska. While most migrate south, some stay and are commonly seen in winter. Often seen in flocks with chickadees, woodpeckers and Ruby-crowned Kinglets. Flicks its wings when moving around. Builds an unusual hanging nest, usually with moss, lichens and spider webs, and lines it with bark and feathers. Can have so many eggs in its small nest that eggs are in two layers. Drinks tree sap and feeds by gleaning insects from trees. Can be very tame and approachable.

Ruby-crowned Kinglet
Regulus calendula

Size: 4" (10 cm)

Male: Small, teardrop-shaped green-to-gray bird. Two white wing bars and a white eye-ring. Hidden ruby crown.

Female: same as male, but lacking the ruby crown

Juvenile: same as female

Nest: pendulous; female builds; 1 brood per year

Eggs: 4-5; white with brown markings

Incubation: 11-12 days; female incubates

Fledging: 11-12 days; female and male feed young

Migration: complete, to western states, Mexico and Central America

Food: insects, berries

Compare: The Golden-crowned Kinglet (pg. 227) is similar, but lacks a ruby crown. The Arctic Warbler (pg. 231) is larger than the Ruby-crowned Kinglet and has eyebrows.

Stan's Notes: One of the smaller birds in Alaska. It takes a quick eye to see the male's ruby crown. A summer resident that is most commonly seen during migration, when groups travel together. Look for it flitting around thick shrubs low to the ground. Female builds an unusual pendulous (sac-like) nest, intricately woven and decorated on the outside with colored lichens and mosses stuck together with spider webs. The nest is suspended from a branch overlapped by leaves and usually is hung high in a mature tree. The common name "Kinglet" comes from the Anglo-Saxon word *cyning*, or "king," referring to the male's ruby crown, and the diminutive suffix "let," meaning "small."

Arctic Warbler
Phylloscopus borealis

SUMMER

Size: 5" (13 cm)

Male: Dull olive green-gray warbler. Long, narrow light line from the base of bill over each eye, extending nearly to the back of head. Small, very narrow wing bars. Bill is gray to dirty yellow. Pale yellow legs and feet.

Female: same as male

Juvenile: similar to adult

Nest: cup, with a dome covering (oven); female builds; 1 brood per year

Eggs: 4-7; pale white with reddish brown-to-pink markings

Incubation: 10-14 days; female incubates

Fledging: 18-20 days; female and male feed young

Migration: complete, to Philippines, East Indies, Asia

Food: insects

Compare: Ruby-crowned Kinglet (pg. 229) is smaller and lacks eyebrows. The Golden-crowned Kinglet (pg. 227) is also smaller and has a distinctive black and yellowish crown.

Stan's Notes: Actually a member of the Old World warbler group. Represents a diverse Eurasian group that reaches North America by crossing the Bering Sea to reach Alaska. Usually found along river-banks in low, dense willow vegetation. Male perches and sings to attract a mate. Female uses dried grasses to build a unique dome-shaped nest (oven) with an entrance hole on one side, and lines it with fine grass and animal hair. Often nests on the ground under a shrub. Feeds heavily on the abundant insects in Alaska in summer.

YEAR-ROUND

Black-capped Chickadee
Poecile atricapillus

Size: 5" (13 cm)

Male: Familiar gray bird with black cap and throat patch. White chest. Tan belly. Small white wing marks.

Female: same as male

Juvenile: same as adult

Nest: cavity; female and male build or excavate; 1 brood per year

Eggs: 5-7; white with fine brown markings

Incubation: 11-13 days; female and male incubate

Fledging: 14-18 days; female and male feed young

Migration: non-migrator

Food: insects, seeds, fruit; comes to seed and suet feeders

Compare: Similar size as Boreal Chickadee (pg. 235), which has a brown cap. Chestnut-backed Chickadee (pg. 93) is similar in size, but has a distinctive chestnut back.

Stan's Notes: Backyard bird that is attracted to a nest box or seed feeder. Usually the first to find a new feeder. Can be easily tamed and hand fed. Can be a common urban bird since much of its diet comes from bird feeders. Needs to feed each day in winter; forages for food during even the worst winter storms. Usually seen with other birds such as kinglets and woodpeckers. Builds nest mostly with green moss and lines it with animal fur. Name comes from its familiar "chika-dee-dee-dee-dee" call. Will also give a high-pitched, two-toned "fee-bee" call. Can have different calls in various regions.

YEAR-ROUND

Boreal Chickadee
Poecile hudsonica

Size: 5½" (14 cm)

Male: Overall gray with a brown cap, black chin (bib) and light brown sides. White cheeks. Gray extending from cheeks toward nape.

Female: same as male

Juvenile: similar to adult

Nest: cavity; female and male excavate; 1 brood per year

Eggs: 5-8; pale white with brown markings

Incubation: 11-16 days; female incubates

Fledging: 16-18 days; female and male feed young

Migration: non-migrator

Food: seeds, insects; visits seed and suet feeders

Compare: Similar size as the Black-capped Chickadee (pg. 233), which has a black cap. Chestnut-backed Chickadee (pg. 93) is smaller than the Boreal Chickadee and has a distinctive chestnut back.

Stan's Notes: A common and widespread chickadee species in the southern two-thirds of Alaska. Like other chickadees, the Boreal is lightweight and has strong feet, allowing it to hang upside down to explore unexploited cracks and crevices for insects. Its wheezy call makes this bird easy to identify, even without seeing it.

female
pg. 103

male

SUMMER

Dark-eyed Junco
Junco hyemalis

Size: 5½" (14 cm)

Male: Round, dark-eyed bird with a slate gray-to-charcoal chest, head and back. White belly. Pink bill. Since the outermost tail feathers are white, tail appears as a white V in flight.

Female: same as male, only tan-to-brown color

Juvenile: similar to female, but has a streaked breast and head

Nest: cup; female and male construct; 2 broods per year

Eggs: 3-5; white with reddish brown markings

Incubation: 12-13 days; female incubates

Fledging: 10-13 days; male and female feed young

Migration: complete, throughout the U.S.

Food: seeds, insects; will come to seed feeders

Compare: Rarely confused with any other bird. The Dark-eyed Junco is not in Alaska during the winter. Look for the tiny pink bill and dark head and back to help identify.

Stan's Notes: This is one of Alaska's common summer birds. Nests in a wide variety of wooded habitats in April and May. Adheres to a rigid social hierarchy, with dominant birds chasing less dominant birds. Look for its white outer tail feathers flashing while in flight. Most comfortable on the ground, juncos will "double-scratch" with both feet to expose seeds and insects. Consumes many weed seeds. Usually seen on the ground in small flocks. Females tend to migrate farther south than the males. Several junco species have now been combined into one, simply called Dark-eyed Junco.

male

first winter

female

Yellow-rumped Warbler
Dendroica coronata

Size: 5-6" (13-15 cm)

Male: Slate gray bird with black streaks on breast. Yellow patches on rump, flanks and head. White chin and belly. Two white wing bars.

Female: duller than male, but same yellow patches

Juvenile: similar to female

Nest: cup; female builds; 2 broods per year

Eggs: 4-5; white with brown markings

Incubation: 12-13 days; female incubates

Fledging: 10-12 days; female and male feed young

Migration: complete, to western states, Mexico and Central America

Food: insects, berries; rarely comes to suet feeders

Compare: Male Yellow Warbler (pg. 363) is all yellow with orange streaks on the breast. The male Wilson's Warbler (pg. 359) has a black cap

Stan's Notes: A summer resident in most of Alaska, with flocks of hundreds seen during migration. Nests in coniferous and aspen forests. Male molts to a dull color in winter similar to the female and retains the yellow patches. Frequently called Myrtle Warbler in eastern states and Audubon's Warbler in western states. Sometimes called Butter-butts due to the yellow patch on rump. Familiar call is a single robust "chip," heard mostly during migration. Also has a wonderful song in spring.

SUMMER

Bluethroat
Luscinia svecica

Size: 6" (15 cm)

Male: A gray bird with a bright blue chin, throat and upper breast. Rusty mark in center of throat and rust on the upper breast. White lower breast and belly. White eyebrows.

Female: similar to male, with less blue and a white chin and throat

Juvenile: similar to female, lacks blue and rust

Nest: cup; female and male construct; 1 brood per year

Eggs: 4-7; green with reddish brown markings

Incubation: 12-15 days; female incubates

Fledging: 10-14 days; female and male feed young

Migration: complete, to Southeast Asia, the Near East and Africa

Food: insects, seeds, berries

Compare: Male Northern Wheatear (pg. 243) is the same size, but has a black mask and wings. Look for Bluethroat's blue and rust marks to identify.

Stan's Notes: Eurasian species found only in Alaska for the short summer months. Widely distributed in the Eurasian Arctic. Found in dense vegetation, where the male sings from prominent perches to attract a mate. Courting male throws its head back, cocks its tail and droop its wings while moving around the female and singing. Usually nests on the ground, constructing a cup nest of grass, roots, moss and lined with fine plant materials. Feeds mainly on insects. After the eggs hatch, both parents care for the young.

male

female

MIGRATION
SUMMER

Northern Wheatear
Oenanthe oenanthe

Size: 6" (15 cm)

Male: A gray bird with black wings and tip of tail. Black mark through eyes, appearing like a mask. Tan mark near the side of the head, extending toward the upper breast. Nearly white belly. White rump and undertail.

Female: similar to male, lacks the black mask

Juvenile: similar to female, lacks black wings

Nest: cavity; female and male construct; 1 brood per year

Eggs: 4-7; pale blue to white without markings

Incubation: 12-15 days; female and male incubate

Fledging: 15-16 days; female and male feed young

Migration: complete, to China, Mongolia, India, Africa

Food: insects, seeds, berries

Compare: Same size as the male Bluethroat (pg. 241), which has a bright blue throat and upper breast. Look for the black mask and wings of male Northern Wheatear to help identify.

Stan's Notes: A Eurasian species seen only throughout Alaska and in parts of Canada in summer. Found in open tundra habitat with abundant rock piles or exposed cliffs. Nests in cavities underneath rocks, often in deserted mammal burrows. Builds nest from grass, roots and moss and lines it with fine plant material. Feeds mainly on insects. Male courts female by hopping and bowing around her with his tail fanned. Male will also sing a flight song before gliding down with tail fanned. Parents divide their brood 3-4 days after fledging, with each parent feeding its half of the young.

Western Wood-Pewee
Contopus sordidulus

Size: 6" (15 cm)

Male: An overall gray bird with darker wings and tail. Two narrow gray wing bars. Dull white throat with pale yellow or white belly. Black upper bill, dull orange lower.

Female: same as male

Juvenile: similar to adult, lacking the two-toned bill

Nest: cup; female builds; 1 brood per year

Eggs: 2-4; pale white with brown markings

Incubation: 12-14 days; female incubates

Fledging: 14-18 days; female and male feed young

Migration: complete, to Central and South America

Food: insects

Compare: Say's Phoebe (pg. 251) is larger and has a tawny belly.

Stan's Notes: Nesting bird in the southeastern quarter of the state. Breeds throughout western North America from Alaska to Mexico. Most common in aspen forests and places near water. Needs trees with dead tops or branches from which to sing and hunt for flying insects, which compose nearly all of its diet. Frequently returns to the same perch after each foray. Overall populations are decreasing about 1 percent each year. The common name comes from its nasal whistle, "pee-wee."

breeding
pg. 115

non-breeding

MIGRATION
SUMMER

Least Sandpiper
Calidris minutilla

Size: 6" (15 cm)

Male: Non-breeding is overall gray to light brown with a distinct brown breast band and light gray eyebrows. White belly and dull yellow legs. Short, down-curved black bill.

Female: same as male

Juvenile: similar to non-breeding adult, but is buffy brown and lacks the breast band

Nest: ground; male and female construct; 1 brood per year

Eggs: 3-4; olive with dark markings

Incubation: 19-23 days; male and female incubate

Fledging: 25-28 days; male and female feed young

Migration: complete, to California, Mexico and Central America

Food: aquatic and terrestrial insects, seeds

Compare: Often confused with non-breeding Western Sandpiper (pg. 249). The Least Sandpiper's yellow legs differentiate it from other tiny sandpipers. The short, thin, down-curved bill also helps to identify.

Stan's Notes: The smallest of the peeps (sandpipers). This is a tame bird that can be approached without scaring. Nests on the Alaskan tundra. Seen in the southern three-quarters of the state in summer and during migration. Prefers the grassy flats of saltwater and freshwater ponds. The yellow legs can be hard to see in water, poor light or when covered with mud.

breeding
pg. 117

non-breeding

MIGRATION
SUMMER

Western Sandpiper
Calidris mauri

Size: 6½" (16 cm)

Male: Non-breeding plumage is dull gray to light brown overall. White belly and eyebrows. Black legs. Narrow bill that droops near tip.

Female: same as male

Juvenile: similar to breeding adult, bright buff brown on the back only

Nest: ground; male and female construct; 1 brood per year

Eggs: 2-4; light brown with dark markings

Incubation: 20-22 days; male and female incubate

Fledging: 19-21 days; male and female feed young

Migration: complete, to California, Mexico and Central America

Food: aquatic and terrestrial insects

Compare: Non-breeding Least Sandpiper (pg. 247) is very similar, but the Western Sandpiper has black legs and a longer bill that droops slightly at the tip. Non-breeding Red Knot (pg. 273) has barring on the flanks.

Stan's Notes: Summer resident along the western coast of Alaska, nesting on the tundra in large "loose" colonies. Feeds on insects at the water's edge, sometimes immersing its head. Young leave the nest (precocial) within a few hours after hatching. Female leaves and the male tends the hatchlings. A long-distance migrant, with adults leaving the breeding grounds several weeks before young.

Say's Phoebe
Sayornis saya

Size: 7½" (19 cm)

Male: Overall dark gray, darkest on head, tail and wings. Belly and undertail tawny. Black bill.

Female: same as male

Juvenile: similar to adult, but browner overall with 2 tawny wing bars and a yellow lower bill

Nest: cup; female builds; 1-2 broods per year

Eggs: 3-6; pale white with brown markings

Incubation: 12-14 days; female incubates

Fledging: 14-16 days; female and male feed young

Migration: complete, to California, Mexico and Central and South America

Food: insects, berries

Compare: Western Wood-Pewee (pg. 245) is smaller and lacks a tawny belly.

Stan's Notes: A widespread nester across Alaska below 9,000-foot (2,750 m) elevations. Nests in cliff crevices, abandoned buildings, bridges and other vertical structures. Usually uses its nest several times each season, returning the following year to the same nest. A nearly all-insect diet. Flies out from a perch to grab an aerial insect and returns to the same perch (hawking). Also hunts insects on the ground, hovering and dropping down to catch them. Phoebes are classified as New World Flycatchers and are not related to the Old World Flycatchers. Was named after Thomas Say, who is said to have discovered this bird in Colorado. The genus, species and first part of its common name refer to Mr. Say. Common name "Phoebe" is likely an imitation of the bird's call.

American Dipper
Cinclus mexicanus

YEAR-ROUND

Size: 7½" (19 cm)

Male: Dark gray to black overall. Head is slightly lighter in color. A short upturned tail. Dark eyes and bill.

Female: same as male

Juvenile: similar to adult, only paler with white eyelids that are most noticeable when blinking

Nest: pendulous, covered nest with the entrance near the bottom, on cliff, behind waterfall; female builds; 1-2 broods per year

Eggs: 3-5; white without markings

Incubation: 13-17 days; female incubates

Fledging: 18-25 days; female and male feed young

Migration: non-migrator; will seek moving open water during winter

Food: aquatic insects, small fish, crustaceans

Compare: Similar shape as American Robin (pg. 265), but lacks a red breast. The only songbird in Alaska that dives into fast-moving water.

Stan's Notes: A common bird of fast, usually noisy streams that provide some kind of protected shelf on which to construct a nest. Some have had success attracting with man-made ledges. Plunges headfirst into fast-moving water, looking for just about any aquatic insect, propelling itself underwater with its wings. Frequently seen emerging with a large insect, which it smashes against rock before eating. Has the ability to fly directly into the air from underwater. Depending on snowmelt, nesting usually starts in March or April. Dippers in lower elevations often nest a second time each season.

female

male

non-breeding
male

Red-necked Phalarope
Phalaropus lobatus

SUMMER

Size: 8" (20 cm)

Female: Overall gray bird with a wide black stripe from base of bill across eyes and down the face. Rusty red neck. White chin and sides of body. Thin black bill. Long dark legs.

Male: similar to female, but duller and less red

Juvenile: similar to male, lacks the rusty red neck

Nest: ground; male builds; 1 brood per year

Eggs: 2-4; olive with brown markings

Incubation: 17-21 days; male incubates

Fledging: 18-21 days; male teaches young to feed

Migration: complete, to South America

Food: aquatic insects, seeds, crustaceans, mollusks

Compare: Smaller than the non-breeding Short-billed Dowitcher (pg. 271) and has a much shorter bill. Smaller than the breeding Red Knot (pg. 327), which has a rusty red neck, chest and belly.

Stan's Notes: Female is brighter than male, and the sex roles are reversed. Some females mate with many males (polyandrous) and lay eggs. Female abandons male once eggs are laid. Male builds a ground nest along tundra ponds, often under a low shrub, and lines it with grass and moss. Male incubates with a brood patch, a bare area on the belly that keeps eggs close to the body for incubation, something only females usually have. Young hatch at the same time and swim within hours of birth. Males often adopt orphans. Doesn't dive underwater to feed, but swims about like a wind-up toy, often spinning in circles, quickly picking up insects stirred to the surface.

breeding
pg. 139

non-breeding

Dunlin
Calidris alpina

Size: 8-9" (20-22.5 cm)

Male: Non-breeding adult has a light gray breast, brownish gray back and white belly. Stout bill, curving slightly downward at the tip. Black legs.

Female: slightly larger than male, with a longer bill

Juvenile: slightly rusty back with a spotty breast

Nest: ground; male and female construct; 1 brood per year

Eggs: 2-4; olive buff or blue green with red brown markings

Incubation: 21-22 days; male and female incubate, male incubates during the day, female at night

Fledging: 19-21 days; male feeds young, female often leaves before young fledge

Migration: complete, to western coastal U.S., Mexico and Central America

Food: insects

Compare: The non-breeding Dunlin is overall gray and has a stout down-curved bill.

Stan's Notes: Non-breeding plumage usually seen from August to early May. Breeding plumage more commonly seen during spring. Flights include heights of up to 100 feet (30 m) with brief gliding alternating with shallow flutters, and a rhythmic, repeating song. Huge flocks fly synchronously, with birds twisting and turning, flashing light and dark undersides. Males tend to fly farther south in winter than females.

Townsend's Solitaire
Myadestes townsendi

Size: 8½" (22 cm)

Male: All-gray robin look-alike with a prominent white ring around each eye. Wings slightly darker than the body. Long tail. Short dark bill and dark legs.

Female: same as male

Juvenile: darker gray with a tan scaly appearance

Nest: cup; female builds; 1-2 broods per year

Eggs: 3-5; blue, green, gray or white with brown markings

Incubation: 12-14 days; female incubates

Fledging: 10-14 days; female and male feed young

Migration: complete, to southwestern states, Mexico; known to migrate to eastern states

Food: insects, fruit

Compare: American Robin (pg. 265) has a red breast. Gray Jay (pg. 279) has a white head.

Stan's Notes: A summer resident of coniferous mountain forests. "Hawks" for insects, perching in trees and darting out to capture them. During winter, eats berries when insects are not available and actively defends a good berry source from other birds. Builds nest on the ground sheltered by rocks or an overhang, or occasionally low in a tree or shrub. Song is a series of clear flute-like whistles without a distinct pattern. Shows white outer tail feathers and light tan patches on wings when in flight.

male pg. 7

female

Rusty Blackbird
Euphagus carolinus

Size: 9" (22.5 cm)

Female: Overall gray blackbird with rusty edges of feathers. Yellow eyes. A short, thin pointed bill. Non-breeding is much browner with a gray rump and black patch around each eye.

Male: glossy black blackbird with blue and purple highlights, bright yellow eyes, a short, thin pointed bill, non-breeding plumage is more rusty brown than glossy black

Juvenile: similar to female

Nest: cup; female builds; 1-2 broods per year

Eggs: 4-5; bluish with brown markings

Incubation: 12-14 days; female incubates

Fledging: 11-13 days; male and female feed young

Migration: complete, to eastern states

Food: insects, seeds

Compare: Female Red-winged Blackbird (pg. 137) is slightly smaller and heavily streaked, with prominent white eyebrows.

Stan's Notes: This bird nests across most of Alaska in small loose colonies, often preferring more wooded, swampy areas. Male feeds female while she incubates. Gathers in large groups. Flocks with other blackbirds to migrate in autumn. When in flight, the end of tail often appears squared.

male pg. 325

female

Pine Grosbeak
Pinicola enucleator

YEAR-ROUND
SUMMER

Size: 9" (22.5 cm)

Female: Plump gray finch with a long dark tail and dark wings. Two white wing bars. Head and rump are tinged dull yellow. Short, stubby, pointed dark bill.

Male: overall rosy red and gray

Juvenile: female is similar to adult female, male has a touch of red on head and rump

Nest: cup; female builds; 1 brood per year

Eggs: 4-5; bluish green without markings

Incubation: 13-15 days; female incubates

Fledging: 13-20 days; female and male feed young

Migration: non-migrator to irruptive; moves around in winter to find food

Food: seeds, fruit, insects; will come to feeders

Compare: Female Red Crossbill (pg. 367) and female White-winged Crossbill (pg. 369) are much smaller and have a crossed bill.

Stan's Notes: This finch is common in Alaska in some years and not so common in others. Very tame and approachable bird. Often seen along roads or on the ground, eating tiny grains of sand and dirt to aid digestion. Seed eater that favors coniferous woods, rarely moving out of coniferous regions in summer. Often seen bathing in fluffy snow. Flies with a typical finch-like undulating pattern while calling a soft whistle. During the breeding season, male and female develop a pouch in the bottom of the mouth (buccal pouch) to transport seeds to young. Male sings a beautiful rich song all year.

263

SUMMER

American Robin
Turdus migratorius

Size: 9-11" (22.5-28 cm)

Male: A familiar gray bird with a rusty red breast and nearly black head and tail. White chin with black streaks. White eye-ring.

Female: similar to male, but with a gray head and a duller breast

Juvenile: similar to female, but has a speckled breast and brown back

Nest: cup; female builds with help from the male; 2-3 broods per year

Eggs: 4-7; pale blue without markings

Incubation: 12-14 days; female incubates

Fledging: 14-16 days; female and male feed young

Migration: complete, to western states, Mexico and Central America

Food: insects, fruit, berries, worms

Compare: Familiar bird to all.

Stan's Notes: Can be heard singing all night long during spring. Most people don't realize how easy it is to differentiate between the male and female robins. Compare the male's dark, nearly black head and brick red breast with the female's gray head and dull red breast. A robin is not listening for worms when cocking its head to one side. It is looking with eyes placed far back on the sides of its head. This is a very territorial bird, often seen fighting its own reflection in windows.

YEAR-ROUND
SUMMER
WINTER

Northern Shrike
Lanius excubitor

Size: 10" (25 cm)

Male: Overall gray bird with black wings and tail. Distinctive black mask across eyes. A small white patch on black wings, seen in flight. Large black bill with a hooked tip.

Female: same as male

Juvenile: tan to light brown overall with dark wings, finely streaked chest

Nest: cup; female and male construct; 1 brood per year

Eggs: 4-6; gray to olive green with brown marks

Incubation: 15-16 days; female incubates

Fledging: 18-20 days; female and male feed young

Migration: complete, to southeastern Alaska, northern states

Food: large insects, small mammals, small birds

Compare: Gray Jay (pg. 279) is larger and lacks the black mask and wings. Look for the black mask and large black bill with a hooked tip to help identify the Northern Shrike.

Stan's Notes: Songbird that acts like a bird of prey. Often seen out in the open, where it sits still for long periods of time watching for prey movement. Unlike a bird of prey, its feet aren't strong enough to hold prey still while it eats. Skewers large insects, mice and other prey on barbed wire fences, long thorns or other sharp objects to hold prey still while tearing it apart. For this reason, it is also called Butcher Bird. Winter populations and migratory behavior may be influenced by the availability of food.

Surfbird
Aphriza virgata

MIGRATION
SUMMER
WINTER

Size: 10" (25 cm)

Male: Breeding (Mar-Aug) is gray with dark spots and a tan-to-brown wash on upper wings and back. White belly. Yellow legs and feet. Winter (Jul-Apr) is gray with a white belly. Distinctive black-tipped white tail. White wing linings, seen in flight anytime of year.

Female: same as male

Juvenile: similar to winter adult

Nest: ground; female and male construct; 1 brood per year

Eggs: 1-4; pale tan with brown markings

Incubation: 22-24 days; female and male incubate

Fledging: 19-24 days; female and male feed young

Migration: complete, to southeastern coastal Alaska, western coastal U.S. and Mexico

Food: aquatic insects, mussels, barnacles, seeds, crustaceans

Compare: Slightly larger than the breeding Ruddy Turnstone (pg. 37), which has a black and white face. The breeding Red Knot (pg. 327) has a salmon head, chest and belly.

Stan's Notes: Nests along rocky alpine ridges above the tree line in Alaska. Winters in small flocks of under 20 individuals. Feeding birds give high squeaks to keep in contact with the flock. Usually difficult for people to hear these birds due to loud crashing surf. Has three different breeding vocalizations: songs, calls and laughs. Male performs display flights of long gliding phases while calling.

breeding
pg. 143

non-breeding

MIGRATION
SUMMER

Short-billed Dowitcher
Limnodromus griseus

Size: 11" (28 cm)

Male: Non-breeding plumage back and wings are gray to light brown. White belly. Off-white eyebrow stripe. A long, straight black bill. Dull yellow-to-green legs and feet.

Female: same as male

Juvenile: similar to non-breeding adult

Nest: ground; female and male construct; 1 brood per year

Eggs: 3-4; olive green with dark markings

Incubation: 20-21 days; male and female incubate

Fledging: 25-27 days; male and female feed young

Migration: complete, to coastal Mexico

Food: insects, snails, worms, leeches, seeds

Compare: Non-breeding Black-bellied Plover (pg. 277) is similar in size, but has a tiny bill unlike the long bill of the Short-billed Dowitcher. The non-breeding Red Knot (pg. 273) lacks the dark patch on head and has a shorter bill. Red-necked Phalarope (pg. 255) is smaller and has a much shorter bill.

Stan's Notes: Summer resident seen along southern coastal Alaska and inland on freshwater lakes and marshes. With a rapid probing action like a sewing machine, it uses its long straight bill to probe deep into sand and mud for insects.

271

breeding
pg. 327

non-breeding

Red Knot
Calidris canutus

MIGRATION
SUMMER

Size: 11" (28 cm)

Male: Non-breeding (Sep-Apr) is overall gray with dark wing tips and dark barring on white flanks. Medium length straight black bill.

Female: same as male

Juvenile: overall gray with white eyebrows and dull yellow legs

Nest: ground; male and female construct; 1 brood per year

Eggs: 3-4; olive with brown markings

Incubation: 21-23 days; male and female incubate

Fledging: 18-20 days; female and male feed young

Migration: complete, to coastal California, Mexico and Central and South America

Food: insects, mollusks, snails, marine worms, small fish

Compare: The non-breeding Short-billed Dowitcher (pg. 271) has a longer bill, dark patch on head and feeds by probing into mud like a sewing machine. The non-breeding Western Sandpiper (pg. 247) lacks barring on flanks.

Stan's Notes: One of the longest migrating shorebirds, nesting on the Arctic tundra and wintering as far south as Tierra del Fuego, Argentina. Stops in coastal North America. Feeds in large flocks of up to 100 individuals, often with other shorebirds. Usually is seen standing on one leg on the beach, resting between feedings. Was the most abundant shorebird in North America; hunting in the late 1800s to early 1900s severely reduced the overall population.

breeding
pg. 41

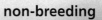

non-breeding

American Golden-Plover
Pluvialis dominica

Size: 11" (28 cm)

Male: Non-breeding plumage (Sep-Apr) is overall gray with white eyebrows and a dark cap. Short dark bill.

Female: same as non-breeding male

Juvenile: similar to non-breeding adult

Nest: ground; male builds; 1 brood per year

Eggs: 3-4; cream with brown markings

Incubation: 26-28 days; male and female incubate

Fledging: 20-22 days; male and female show young what to eat

Migration: complete, to South America

Food: insects, fruit, seeds

Compare: Non-breeding Black-bellied Plover (pg. 277) is similar in size, but has less distinct white eyebrows and a white undertail.

Stan's Notes: This bird was formerly called Lesser Golden-Plover. Was once hunted by market hunters. More than 48,000 birds were reported to have been shot in one day near New Orleans in 1861. Populations were extremely depleted by the early 1900s. May mate for life. Male does most of the nest selection and construction. Male also incubates most of the time. Both sexes feed the young equally.

breeding
pg. 43

non-breeding

MIGRATION
SUMMER

Black-bellied Plover
Pluvialis squatarola

Size: 11-12" (28-30 cm)

Male: Non-breeding is uniformly light gray with dark, nearly black streaks. White belly and chest. Faint white eyebrow mark. Black legs and bill.

Female: less black on belly and breast than male

Juvenile: grayer than adults, with much less black

Nest: ground; male and female construct; 1 brood per year

Eggs: 3-4; pinkish or greenish with black brown markings

Incubation: 26-27 days; male and female incubate, male incubates during the day, female at night

Fledging: 35-45 days; male feeds young, young learn quickly to feed themselves

Migration: complete, to coastal California and Mexico

Food: insects

Compare: The non-breeding American Golden-Plover (pg. 275) lacks the white undertail. The non-breeding Spotted Sandpiper (pg. 131) has a shorter, thicker bill.

Stan's Notes: Male performs a "butterfly" courtship flight to attract females. Female leaves the male and young about 12 days after the eggs hatch. Starts breeding at 3 years of age. Migrant and summer resident along coastal Alaska. In flight, in any plumage, it displays a white rump and stripe on wings with black axillaries (armpits). Often darts across the ground to grab an insect and run.

YEAR-ROUND

Gray Jay
Perisoreus canadensis

Size: 11½" (29 cm)

Male: Large gray bird with a white forehead and nape of neck. Short black bill. Dark eyes.

Female: same as male

Juvenile: sooty gray with a faint white whisker mark

Nest: cup; male and female construct; 1 brood per year

Eggs: 3-4; gray white, finely marked to unmarked

Incubation: 16-18 days; female incubates

Fledging: 14-15 days; male and female feed young

Migration: non-migrator

Food: insects, seeds, fruit, nuts; visits seed feeder

Compare: Slightly larger than the Steller's Jay (pg. 89), but lacks any blue coloring and a crest. The Northern Shrike (pg. 267) is smaller and has a black mask and wings.

Stan's Notes: A bird of coniferous woods in mid to high elevations. Called Camp Robber because it rummages through camps looking for scraps of food. Also known as Whisky Jack or Canada Jay. Easily tamed, it will fly to your hand if offered raisins or nuts. Will eat just about anything. Also stores extra food for winter, balling it together in a sticky mass, placing it on a tree limb, often concealing it with lichen or bark. Travels around in family units of 3-5, making good companions for campers, canoeists and high altitude hikers and climbers. Reminds some of an overgrown chickadee.

soaring

juvenile

soaring
juvenile

Sharp-shinned Hawk
Accipiter striatus

Size: 10-14" (25-36 cm); up to 2-foot wingspan

Male: Small woodland hawk with a gray back and head and a rusty red breast. Long tail with several dark tail bands, widest band at end of squared-off tail. Red eyes.

Female: same as male, only larger

Juvenile: same size as adults, with a brown back and heavily streaked breast, yellow eyes

Nest: platform; female builds; 1 brood per year

Eggs: 4-5; white with brown markings

Incubation: 32-35 days; female incubates

Fledging: 24-27 days; female and male feed young

Migration: complete to non-migrator in Alaska

Food: birds, small mammals

Compare: Much smaller than the Northern Goshawk (pg. 297), which has distinctive white eyebrows. Look for the Sharp-shinned Hawk's squared tail to help identify.

Stan's Notes: A common hawk of backyards and woodlands, often seen swooping in on birds visiting feeders. Its short rounded wings and long tail allow this hawk to navigate through thick stands of trees in pursuit of prey. Common name comes from the sharp keel on the leading edge of its "shin," though it is actually below rather than above the bird's ankle on the tarsus bone of foot.

YEAR-ROUND

Rock Pigeon
Columba livia

Size: 13" (33 cm)

Male: No set color pattern. Gray to white, patches of iridescent greens and blues, usually with a light rump patch.

Female: same as male

Juvenile: same as adult

Nest: platform; female builds; 3-4 broods per year

Eggs: 1-2; white without markings

Incubation: 18-20 days; female and male incubate

Fledging: 25-26 days; female and male feed young

Migration: non-migrator

Food: seeds

Compare: An urban bird familiar to most people and not confused with other birds.

Stan's Notes: Also known as Domestic Pigeon, formerly known as Rock Dove. Introduced to North America from Europe by the early settlers. This bird is most common around cities and barnyards, where it scratches for seeds. One of the few birds that has a wide variety of colors, produced by years of selective breeding while in captivity. Parents feed young (squab) a regurgitated liquid known as crop-milk for the first few days of life. One of the few birds that can drink without tilting its head back. Nests under bridges and on buildings, balconies, barns and sheds. Was once poisoned as a "nuisance city bird." Many cities now have Peregrine Falcons that feed on Rock Pigeons, keeping their numbers in check.

in flight

Long-tailed Jaeger
Stercorarius longicaudus

SUMMER

Size: 15" (38 cm); 8-in. tail; up to 3½-ft. wingspan

Male: A gray bird with darker gray wings and tail. Black cap, nearly white head and short dark bill. Gray legs. Breeding plumage has an extremely long, thin tail.

Female: same as male

Juvenile: dark brown overall with a black-tipped bill

Nest: ground; female and male construct; 1 brood per year

Eggs: 1-2; olive to brown with brown markings

Incubation: 23-25 days; female and male incubate

Fledging: 22-28 days; female and male feed young

Migration: complete, to South America

Food: small mammals and birds, insects, berries

Compare: Parasitic Jaeger (pg. 287) has a brown cap, shorter tail and slightly larger body. Long-tailed is similar in size and shape to many juvenile gulls, but has a black cap. Look for the very long tail to help identify.

Stan's Notes: One of several jaegers species in Alaska. The smallest of the jaegers but has the longest tail, hence its common name. The long tail feathers are molted and replaced with shorter ones for the winter. The nesting biology of all jaeger species is very similar. Has a long-term pair bond, returning to the same region yearly to nest. A ground nester that will actively defend its nest site from intruders, including large mammals. Male defends territory and hunts. Female does most of the incubation and brooding after the eggs hatch.

in
flight

Parasitic Jaeger
Stercorarius parasiticus

SUMMER

Size: 16½" (42 cm); 4-in. tail; up to 3½-ft. wingspan

Male: A gray bird with darker gray wings, tail and legs. A pale yellow-to-white head and neck with a dark brown cap. Short dark bill with a white base. Narrow pointed tail. Small white patch near wing tips, as seen in flight.

Female: same as male

Juvenile: dark brown overall, a black-tipped gray bill

Nest: ground; female and male construct; 1 brood per year

Eggs: 1-2; olive to brown with brown markings

Incubation: 23-28 days; female and male incubate

Fledging: 25-30 days; female and male feed young

Migration: complete, to coastal California, Mexico and Central and South America

Food: birds, eggs, fish, mammals, insects, berries

Compare: Long-tailed Jaeger (pg. 285) has a black cap and longer tail. Juvenile Parasitic Jaeger has a similar size and shape as many juvenile gulls, but has a brown cap. Look for short, pointed central tail feathers and a flash of white near the wing tips when in flight.

Stan's Notes: Often the most common of the jaegers. Usually seen near the coast. Moves out to sea during migration, where it often steals fish from other bird species. Diet is mainly young birds and bird eggs. Sometimes follows predators such as wolves, snatching birds that are distracted by the predator. Has a long-term pair bond.

female pg. 189

male

Gadwall
Anas strepera

YEAR-ROUND
SUMMER

Size: 19" (48 cm)

Male: A plump gray duck with a brown head and a distinctive black rump. White belly and chestnut-tinged wings. Bright white wing linings. Small white wing patch, seen when swimming. Gray bill.

Female: similar to female Mallard, a mottled brown with a pronounced color change from dark brown body to light brown neck and head, bright white wing linings, small white wing patch, gray bill with orange sides

Juvenile: similar to female

Nest: ground; female lines the nest with fine grass and down feathers plucked from her chest; 1 brood per year

Eggs: 8-11; white without markings

Incubation: 24-27 days; female incubates

Fledging: 48-56 days; young feed themselves

Migration: complete to non-migrator in Alaska

Food: aquatic insects

Compare: Male Gadwall is one of the few gray ducks. Look for its distinctive black rump.

Stan's Notes: A duck of shallow marshes. Consumes mostly plant material, dunking its head in water to feed rather than tipping forward, like other dabbling ducks. Walks well on land; feeds in fields and woodlands. Frequently in pairs with other duck species. Nests within 300 feet (100 m) of water. Establishes pair bond in winter.

in
flight

in flight
juvenile

juvenile

YEAR-ROUND
MIGRATION
SUMMER

Peregrine Falcon
Falco peregrinus

Size: 18-20" (45-50 cm); up to 3-foot wingspan

Male: Gray blue back and tail. Breast and under-wings pale white to tan. Some individuals have a wash of salmon on breast. Belly, legs, underwings and undertail are covered with small dark spots, appearing like horizontal bars. Dark head marking ("hood") and a wide black mustache mark. Yellow base of bill, eye-rings and legs.

Female: similar to male, noticeably larger

Juvenile: overall darker than adults, heavy vertical streaks on breast and belly

Nest: ground (scrape), on edge of a cliff; 1 brood per year

Eggs: 3-4; white, occasionally with brown marks

Incubation: 29-32 days; female and male incubate

Fledging: 35-42 days; male and female feed young

Migration: complete to non-migrator in Alaska

Food: birds, Rock Pigeons in many cities

Compare: American Kestrel (pg. 147) is smaller, has 2 vertical black stripes on the face and lacks a dark "hood" and mustache mark.

Stan's Notes: A wide-bodied bird often identified by its dark head marking ("hood"), clear breast and mustache mark. Lives and hunts in cities, diving (stooping) on pigeons at speeds up to 200 miles 322 km) per hour. Rural falcons feed on many species such as shorebirds and waterfowl. Soars with wings flat. Found throughout most of Alaska.

female
pg. 211

male

soaring

juvenile

soaring
juvenile

SUMMER

Northern Harrier
Circus cyaneus

Size: 18½-22½" (47-57 cm); up to 3½-ft. wingspan

Male: A slim, low-flying hawk. Silver gray with a large white rump patch and a white belly. Faint narrow bands across tail. Black wing tips. Yellow eyes.

Female: dark brown back, a brown-streaked breast and belly, large white rump patch, narrow black bands across the tail, black wing tips, yellow eyes

Juvenile: similar to female, with an orange breast

Nest: platform, often on ground; female and male build; 1 brood per year

Eggs: 4-8; bluish white without markings

Incubation: 31-32 days; female incubates

Fledging: 30-35 days; male and female feed young

Migration: complete, to western states and Mexico

Food: mice, snakes, insects, small birds

Compare: Slimmer than Red-tailed Hawk (pg. 213). Look for black tail bands, white rump patch and characteristic flight to help identify.

Stan's Notes: One of the easiest hawks to identify. Harriers glide just above ground, following contours of the land while searching for prey. Holds its wings just above the horizontal position, tilting back and forth in the wind. Formerly called Marsh Hawk due to its habit of hunting over marshes. Feeds on the ground. Will perch on the ground to preen and rest. At any age, has a distinctive owl-like face disk.

in flight

juvenile

Gyrfalcon
Falco rusticolus

Size: 20-25" (50-63 cm); up to 4-foot wingspan

Male: Largest falcon worldwide. Light gray head, back and tail. Dark horizontal barring on a pale white breast and belly. Back and wings have black horizontal barring. Yellow base of bill, eye-rings and legs.

Female: similar to male, noticeably larger

Juvenile: overall light brown with streaking throughout, has two-toned underwings with a paler trailing edge, a wider, longer tail than the adults, bluish cere, eye-rings and legs

Nest: platform, on a cliff edge; female and male construct or take over an old nest; 1 brood per year

Eggs: 3-5; white with brown markings

Incubation: 34-36 days; female and male incubate

Fledging: 49-56 days; male and female feed young

Migration: non-migrator to partial, to northern states

Food: birds (mainly ptarmigan), small mammals

Compare: Peregrine Falcon (pg. 291) is smaller, has a black "hood" and narrower, more pointed wings with darker underwings.

Stan's Notes: A non-migrator and winter resident in Alaska, with some moving farther south in late autumn and winter. Seen only infrequently. Hunts by flying low and capturing prey by surprise. Soars with wings flat. Breeds on rock outcroppings in the Arctic tundra. May skip nesting when prey is scarce. The smaller male does most of the hunting during incubation.

soaring

juvenile

soaring
juvenile

Northern Goshawk
Accipiter gentilis

Size:	21-26" (53-66 cm); up to 3½-foot wingspan
Male:	Blue gray back and upper wings. Light gray breast and belly. Gray underwings with fine dark barring. Black crown. Prominent white eyebrows. Eyes are deep red to mahogany. White undertail coverts. Yellow feet.
Female:	similar to male, noticeably larger, barring on the breast is more coarse
Juvenile:	overall streaked brown with irregular dark bands on tail, yellow eyes
Nest:	platform, in a tree; male and female build; 1 brood per year
Eggs:	2-5; bluish white, sometimes brown marks
Incubation:	36-38 days; female and male incubate
Fledging:	35-42 days; male and female feed young
Migration:	non-migrator to irruptive, to northern states
Food:	birds (especially grouse), small mammals
Compare:	Much larger than the Sharp-shinned Hawk (pg. 281), which has a rusty chest. Look for the gray chest and white undertail coverts of the Northern Goshawk.

Stan's Notes: This is the largest of our woodland accipiters. Hunts by chasing or surprising. Highly dependent on Ruffed Grouse for food; goshawk populations follow grouse populations. Breeds in parts of the lower two-thirds of Alaska, usually beginning at 3 years of age. Female is very aggressive at the nest, boldly attacking. The smaller male hunts smaller prey and feeds the incubating female. Juveniles migrate first.

breeding

winter

Red-throated Loon
Gavia stellata

Size: 25" (63 cm)

Male: Breeding (Apr-Oct) is overall dark brown to nearly black with a gray head and neck and prominent red throat. Long, thin black bill. Winter (Oct-Apr) lacks the red throat, has a white face, neck and breast and a gray back with white spots.

Female: same as male

Juvenile: similar to winter adult

Nest: platform, on the ground; male and female build; 1 brood per year

Eggs: 1-3; brown to olive without markings

Incubation: 24-29 days; female and male incubate

Fledging: 49-51 days; male and female feed young

Migration: complete to non-migrator in Alaska

Food: fish, aquatic insects, amphibians

Compare: Smaller than the breeding Common Loon (pg. 79), which has a black head, a larger, wider bill and lacks the red throat. Winter Common Loon has less white on the neck and face than winter Red-throated Loon.

Stan's Notes: The smallest of loons and the only one that can take flight from dry land rather than by running on the water's surface. Nests on smaller lakes and ponds. Often lays two eggs. Young hatch up to several days apart and ride on backs of swimming adults for their first couple weeks. Less vocal than Common Loon, but gives a short wailing call on breeding grounds. Groups of up to 100 may gather to feed at summer's end; smaller groups migrate during days.

in flight

YEAR-ROUND

Great Gray Owl
Strix nebulosa

Size: 27" (69 cm); up to 4-foot wingspan

Male: Overall gray owl with a large, round puffy head and large, light gray facial disk with a thin black outline. Black and white throat, resembling a bow tie. Yellow eyes.

Female: same as male, only slightly larger

Juvenile: similar to adults, light gray

Nest: platform; takes over a crow or hawk nest or uses a stump or broken-off tree; 1 brood per year

Eggs: 2-4; white without markings

Incubation: 28-30 days; female incubates

Fledging: 21-28 days; male and female feed young

Migration: non-migrator to irruptive; moves around Alaska in winter to find food

Food: small to medium mammals

Compare: Great Horned Owl (pg. 217) is smaller and has ear tufts.

Stan's Notes: Our largest owl. Nests in the southeastern quarter of Alaska. Detects prey beneath snow by sound, plunging into snow to capture. Often hunts along roads during winter to capture mice that have left the cover of snow. This leads to many owl-and-car collisions. One of the more active owls during the day. Not often frightened by human presence. During courtship, male gives 5-10 deep hoots. Female responds with a low whistle or hoot. Some use an artificial nest platform. Young will return to roost in the nest.

in flight

Canada Goose
Branta canadensis

Size: 25-43" (63-109 cm); up to 5½-foot wingspan

Male: Large gray goose with a black neck and head and a white chin or cheek strap.

Female: same as male

Juvenile: same as adult

Nest: platform, on the ground; female constructs; 1 brood per year

Eggs: 5-10; white without markings

Incubation: 25-30 days; female incubates

Fledging: 42-55 days; male and female teach young to feed

Migration: complete, to western states

Food: aquatic plants, insects, seeds

Compare: Similar size as the Brant (pg. 77), which has a white necklace and lacks Canada Goose's white cheek strap.

Stan's Notes: Summer resident in most of Alaska and seen during migration. Adults mate for many years, but only start to breed in their third year. Males frequently act as sentinels, standing at the edge of the group, bobbing their heads, becoming very aggressive to anybody who approaches. Will hiss as if displaying displeasure. Adults molt primary flight feathers while raising young, rendering family groups flightless at the same time. Several subspecies vary geographically across the U.S. Generally they are darker in color in the western groups and paler in eastern. Size decreases northward, with the smallest subspecies found on the Arctic tundra.

in flight

rusty stain

rusty stain
in flight

Sandhill Crane
Grus canadensis

Size: 40-48" (102-120 cm); up to 7-foot wingspan

Male: Elegant gray bird with long legs and neck. Wings and body often stained rusty brown. Scarlet red cap. Yellow-to-red eyes.

Female: same as male

Juvenile: dull brown, lacks red cap, has yellow eyes

Nest: platform, on the ground; female and male build; 1 brood per year

Eggs: 2; olive with brown markings

Incubation: 28-32 days; female and male incubate

Fledging: 65 days; female and male feed young

Migration: complete, to southwestern states, Mexico

Food: insects, fruit, worms, plants, amphibians

Compare: A tall, long-legged gray bird that is not confused with other birds. Look for Sandhill Crane's scarlet red cap to help identify.

Stan's Notes: Among the tallest birds in the world and capable of flying at great heights. Usually seen in large undisturbed fields near water. Has a very distinctive rattling call. Often heard before seen. Plumage often appears rusty brown (see insets) due to staining from mud during preening. A characteristic flight with upstroke quicker than down. Performing a spectacular mating dance, the birds face each other, bow and jump into the air while uttering loud cackling sounds and flapping wings. Often flips sticks and grass into the air during dance.

male

female

Violet-green Swallow
Tachycineta thalassina

Size: 5¼" (13.5 cm)

Male: Dull emerald green crown, nape and back. Violet blue wings and tail. White chest and belly. White cheeks with white extending above the eyes. Wings extend beyond the tail when perching.

Female: same as male, only duller

Juvenile: similar to adult of the same sex

Nest: cavity; female and male construct; 1 brood per year

Eggs: 4-6; pale white with brown markings

Incubation: 13-14 days; female incubates

Fledging: 18-24 days; female and male feed young

Migration: complete, to Central and South America

Food: insects

Compare: Similar size as the Cliff Swallow (pg. 101), which has a distinctive tan-to-rust pattern on the head. Barn Swallow (pg. 85) has a distinctive, deeply forked tail.

Stan's Notes: A solitary nester in tree cavities, but rarely under cliff overhangs, unlike colony-nesting Cliff Swallows. Can be attracted with a nest box. Will search for miles for errant feathers to line nest. A short tail with wing tips extending beyond the end of tail when perching. Returns to Alaska in late April and begins nesting in May. Young often leave nest by June.

female pg. 205

male

Mallard
Anas platyrhynchos

Size: 20½" (52 cm)

Male: Large, bulbous green head, white necklace and rust brown or chestnut chest. Gray and white on the sides. Yellow bill. Orange legs and feet.

Female: brown duck with an orange and black bill and blue and white wing mark (speculum)

Juvenile: same as female, but with a yellow bill

Nest: ground; female builds; 1 brood per year

Eggs: 7-10; greenish to whitish, unmarked

Incubation: 26-30 days; female incubates

Fledging: 42-52 days; female leads young to food

Migration: complete to non-migrator in parts of Alaska

Food: seeds, plants, aquatic insects; will come to ground feeders offering corn

Compare: Male Red-breasted Merganser (pg. 313) has a shaggy crest and an orange bill. The male Northern Shoveler (pg. 311) has a white chest with rust on sides and a dark spoon-shaped bill. Male Northern Pintail (pg. 207) has long tail feathers and a brown head.

Stan's Notes: A familiar duck of lakes and ponds, it's considered a type of dabbling duck, tipping forward in shallow water to feed on aquatic plants on the bottom. The name "Mallard" comes from the Latin *masculus*, meaning "male," referring to the habit of males not taking part in raising ducklings. Black central tail feathers of male curl upward. Both the male and female have white tails and white underwings. Will return to place of birth.

YEAR-ROUND
MIGRATION
SUMMER
WINTER

female pg. 209

male

Northern Shoveler
Anas clypeata

SUMMER

Size: 20½" (52 cm)

Male: Medium-sized duck with iridescent green head, rusty sides and white breast. Has an extraordinarily large spoon-shaped bill that is almost always held pointed toward water.

Female: brown and black all over, blue wing patch, spoon-shaped bill

Juvenile: same as female

Nest: ground; female builds; 1 brood per year

Eggs: 9-12; olive without markings

Incubation: 22-25 days; female incubates

Fledging: 30-60 days; female leads young to food

Migration: complete, to southwestern states, Mexico

Food: aquatic insects, plants

Compare: Similar to male Mallard (pg. 209), but the Northern Shoveler has a large, characteristic spoon-shaped bill.

Stan's Notes: One of several species of shoveler, so called because of the peculiar shape of its bill. The first part of the common name was given because this is the only species of these ducks in North America. Found in small flocks of 5-10 birds, swimming low in water with its large bill pointed toward the water, as if it's too heavy to lift. Feeds mainly by filtering tiny aquatic insects and plants from the water's surface with its bill.

female pg. 219

male

Red-breasted Merganser
Mergus serrator

YEAR-ROUND
SUMMER

Size: 23" (58 cm)

Male: A shaggy green head and crest. Prominent white collar. Rusty breast. Black and white body. Long orange bill.

Female: overall brown to gray with a shaggy reddish head and crest, long orange bill

Juvenile: similar to female

Nest: ground; female builds; 1 brood per year

Eggs: 5-10; olive green without markings

Incubation: 29-30 days; female incubates

Fledging: 55-65 days; female feeds young

Migration: complete to non-migrator in Alaska

Food: fish, aquatic insects

Compare: Smaller than the male Common Merganser (pg. 315), which has white sides and breast and lacks a crest.

Stan's Notes: Breeding resident in Alaska. The most widespread of summer mergansers, arriving in April and leaving in October. Most commonly seen along the southeastern Alaska coast, but can also be seen in large inland freshwater lakes. A very fast flier, clocked at up to 100 miles (161 km) per hour. Usually seen flying low across the water. Needs a long run for takeoff with wings flapping to get airborne. Serrated bill helps it catch slippery fish. Usually a silent duck. Male occasionally gives a soft, catlike meow. Female gives a harsh "krrr-croak." Does not breed before 2 years. Male abandons female just after eggs are laid. Females will often share nests. Young leave the nest within 24 hours of hatching, never to return.

in flight

female pg. 331

male

SUMMER

Common Merganser
Mergus merganser

Size: 27" (69 cm)

Male: Long, thin, duck-like bird with green head, a black back, and white sides, breast and neck. Has a long, pointed orange bill. Often appears to be black and white in poor light.

Female: same size and shape as the male, but with a rusty red head, ragged "hair" on head, gray body with white chest and chin, and long, pointed orange bill

Juvenile: same as female

Nest: cavity; female lines old woodpecker cavity; 1 brood per year

Eggs: 9-11; ivory without markings

Incubation: 28-33 days; female incubates

Fledging: 70-80 days; female feeds young

Migration: complete, to western states and Mexico

Food: small fish, aquatic insects

Compare: Male Mallard (pg. 309) is smaller and lacks the black back and long pointed bill. Male Red breasted Merganser (pg. 313) is smaller and lacks the white sides and chest.

Stan's Notes: The merganser is a shallow water diver that feeds on small fish in 10-15 feet (3-4.5 m) of water. More commonly seen along rivers than lakes. The bill has a fine serrated-like edge to help catch slippery fish. Females often lay eggs in other merganser nests (egg dumping), resulting in broods of up to 15 young per mother. Male leaves the female when she starts to incubate eggs. Orphans are accepted by other merganser mothers with young.

Rufous Hummingbird
Selasphorus rufus

SUMMER

Size: 3¾" (9.5 cm)

Male: Tiny burnt orange bird with a black throat patch (gorget) that reflects orange-red in sunlight. White chest. Green-to-tan flanks.

Female: same as male, but lacking the throat patch

Juvenile: similar to female

Nest: cup; female builds; 1-2 broods per year

Eggs: 1-3; white without markings

Incubation: 14-17 days; female incubates

Fledgling: 21-26 days; female feeds young

Migration: complete, to Central and South America

Food: nectar, insects; will come to nectar feeders

Compare: The only regularly occurring hummingbird found in Alaska. Identify it by the unique orange-red (rufous) color.

Stan's Notes: One of the smallest birds in the state. This is a bold, hardy hummer. Frequently seen well out of its normal range in the western U.S., showing up along the East coast. Visits hummingbird feeders in your yard during migration. Does not sing, but it will chatter or buzz to communicate. Weighing just 2-3 grams, it takes about five average-sized hummingbirds to equal the weight of one chickadee. The heart pumps an incredible 1,260 beats per minute. Male performs a spectacular pendulum-like flight over the perched female. After mating, the female will fly off to build a nest and raise young, without any help from her mate. Constructs a soft, flexible nest that expands to accommodate the growing young.

Varied Thrush
Ixoreus naevius

SUMMER

Size: 9½" (24 cm)

Male: Potbellied robin-like bird with orange eyebrows, chin, breast and wing bars. Head, neck and back are gray to blue. Black breast band and eye mark.

Female: browner version of male, lacking the black breast band

Juvenile: similar to female

Nest: cup; female builds; 1-2 broods per year

Eggs: 3-5; pale blue with brown markings

Incubation: 12-14 days; female incubates

Fledging: 10-15 days; female and male feed young

Migration: complete, to western states

Food: insects, fruit

Compare: Similar size and shape as American Robin (pg. 265), but Varied Thrush has a warm orange breast unlike the red breast of the Robin. The Varied Thrush has a distinctive black breast band.

Stan's Notes: This intriguing-looking bird nests in the southern two-thirds of Alaska. Prefers moist coniferous forests, but is most common in dense, older coniferous woods in high elevations. In the lower 48 states, it migrates in an east-west pattern. Some birds in western states fly eastward in fall, showing up in nearly any state. Usually is very elusive, feeding on the ground in dense vegetation. Tosses leaves around in search of fallen berries and insects. Gives a distinctive song of long whistles, repeated after a short pause.

female pg. 367

male

Red Crossbill
Loxia curvirostra

YEAR-ROUND

Size: 6½" (16 cm)

Male: Sparrow-sized bird, dirty red to orange with a bright red crown and rump. Dark brown wings. Short dark brown tail. Long, pointed crossed bill.

Female: pale yellow chest, light gray throat patch, a crossed bill, dark brown wings and tail

Juvenile: streaked with tinges of yellow, bill gradually crosses about 2 weeks after fledging

Nest: cup; female builds; 1 brood per year

Eggs: 3-4; bluish white with brown markings

Incubation: 14-18 days; female incubates

Fledging: 16-20 days; female and male feed young

Migration: irruptive; moves around Alaska in winter to find food, will wander as far as Mexico

Food: seeds, leaf buds; comes to seed feeders

Compare: The male White-winged Crossbill (pg. 323) has white wing bars. Male Pine Grosbeak (pg. 325) lacks the crossed bill.

Stan's Notes: The long crossed bill is adapted for extracting seeds from pine and spruce cones, its favorite food. Often dangles upside down like a parrot to reach cones. Also seen on the ground where it eats grit, which helps digest food. Nests in coniferous forests. Some studies show up to nine distinct populations of Red Crossbills, but they are nearly impossible to distinguish in the field. Plumage can be highly variable among individuals. Irruptive behavior makes it more common in some winters and nonexistent in others.

female pg. 369

YEAR-ROUND

White-winged Crossbill
Loxia leucoptera

Size: 6½" (16 cm)

Male: Red-to-pink sparrow-sized bird with black wings and tail. Two large white wing bars. Gray sides and lower belly. A long, slender crossed bill with a dark spot at base (lore).

Female: pale yellow breast with indistinct streaks, dark wings, 2 large white wing bars, dark tail, a long, slender crossed bill

Juvenile: similar to female, the first-year male is pale yellow or pale red

Nest: cup; female builds; 1 brood per year

Eggs: 3-5; pale blue with brown markings

Incubation: 12-14 days; female incubates

Fledging: 16-20 days; female and male feed young

Migration: non-migrator to irruptive; moves around in winter to find food

Food: seeds, berries, insects; comes to seed feeders

Compare: The male Red Crossbill (pg. 321) is very similar to the male White-winged Crossbill, but lacks white wing bars. The male Pine Grosbeak (pg. 325) is much larger and lacks the crossed bill.

Stan's Notes: This bird dangles upside down to reach pine and spruce cones, using its long crossed bill to extracts the seeds. Eats berries and insects to a lesser extent. Usually seen on the ground picking up grit, which helps grind the seeds. Moves around to find a plentiful supply of seeds. Plumage can be highly variable among individuals, with older males more colorful than the younger ones.

male

female pg. 263

Pine Grosbeak
Pinicola enucleator

Size: 9" (22.5 cm)

Male: Plump rosy red and gray finch with a long dark tail. Dark wings with a smattering of gray. Two white wing bars. A short, stubby, pointed dark bill.

Female: mostly gray with dark wings and tail, head and rump are tinged dull yellow

Juvenile: male has a touch of red on head and rump, female is similar to adult female

Nest: cup; female builds; 1 brood per year

Eggs: 4-5; bluish green without markings

Incubation: 13-15 days; female incubates

Fledging: 13-20 days; female and male feed young

Migration: non-migrator to irruptive; moves around in winter to find food

Food: seeds, fruit, insects; will come to feeders

Compare: The male Red Crossbill (pg. 321) and male White-winged Crossbill (pg. 323) are much smaller and have a crossed bill.

Stan's Notes: This finch is common in Alaska in some years and not so common in others. Very tame and approachable bird. Often seen along roads or on the ground, eating tiny grains of sand and dirt to aid digestion. Seed eater that favors coniferous woods, rarely moving out of coniferous regions in summer. Often seen bathing in fluffy snow. Flies with a typical finch-like undulating pattern while calling a soft whistle. During the breeding season, male and female develop a pouch in the bottom of the mouth (buccal pouch) to transport seeds to young. Male sings a beautiful rich song all year.

non-breeding
pg. 273

breeding

MIGRATION
SUMMER

Red Knot
Calidris canutus

Size: 11" (28 cm)

Male: Breeding (May-Aug) has a salmon-colored head, chest and belly. Gray-to-brown back and wings. Medium straight black bill.

Female: same as male

Juvenile: overall gray with white eyebrows and dull yellow legs

Nest: ground; male and female construct; 1 brood per year

Eggs: 3-4; olive with brown markings

Incubation: 21-23 days; male and female incubate

Fledging: 18-20 days; female and male feed young

Migration: complete, to coastal California, Mexico and Central and South America

Food: insects, mollusks, snails, marine worms, small fish

Compare: Breeding Western Sandpiper (pg. 117) has a rusty brown back and a white belly. The breeding Dunlin (pg. 139) has a large black patch on belly. The Whimbrel (pg. 183) has a much longer bill and lacks a reddish belly.

Stan's Notes: One of the longest migrating shorebirds, nesting on the Arctic tundra and wintering as far south as Tierra del Fuego, Argentina. Stops in coastal North America. Feeds in large flocks of up to 100 individuals, often with other shorebirds. Usually is seen standing on one leg on the beach, resting between feedings. Was the most abundant shorebird in North America; hunting in the late 1800s to early 1900s severely reduced the overall population.

female pg. 203

male

Canvasback
Aythya valisineria

SUMMER

Size: 20½" (52 cm)

Male: Deep red head with a sloping forehead that transitions into a long black bill. Red neck. Gray and white sides and back. Black chest and tail.

Female: similar to male, but has a brown head, neck and chest, light gray-to-brown sides and a long dark bill

Juvenile: similar to female

Nest: ground; female builds; 1 brood per year

Eggs: 7-9; pale white to gray without markings

Incubation: 24-29 days; female incubates

Fledging: 56-67 days; female leads young to food

Migration: complete, to western coastal states, Mexico

Food: aquatic insects, small clams

Compare: The male Greater Scaup (pg. 61) and male Lesser Scaup (pg. 51) are smaller, lack the red head and neck of the male Canvasback and have a shorter, light blue bill.

Stan's Notes: A large inland duck of freshwater lakes, rivers and ponds. Populations declined dramatically in the 1960-80s due to marsh drainage for agriculture. Females return to their birthplace (philopatric) while males disperse to new areas. Will mate during migration or on the breeding grounds. A courting male gives a soft cooing call when displaying and during aerial chases. Male leaves the female after incubation starts. Female takes a new mate every year. Female feeds very little during incubation and will lose up to 70 percent of fat reserves during that time.

in flight

male pg. 315

female

Common Merganser

Mergus merganser

Size: 27" (69 cm)

Female: A long, thin, duck-like bird with a rusty red head and ragged "hair" on the back of head. Gray body with white chest and chin. Long, pointed orange bill.

Male: same size and shape as the female, but with a green head, black back, white sides and chest, and long, pointed orange bill

Juvenile: same as female

Nest: cavity; female lines old woodpecker cavity; 1 brood per year

Eggs: 9-11; ivory without markings

Incubation: 28-33 days; female incubates

Fledging: 70-80 days; female feeds young

Migration: complete, to western states and Mexico

Food: small fish, aquatic insects

Compare: Female Red-breasted Merganser (pg. 219) is smaller with a smaller, thinner bill. Look for ragged "hair" on head, a long, pointed orange bill and white chest and chin.

Stan's Notes: The merganser is a shallow water diver that feeds on small fish in 10-15 feet (3-4.5 m) of water. More commonly seen along rivers than lakes. The bill has a fine serrated-like edge to help catch slippery fish. Females often lay eggs in other merganser nests (egg dumping), resulting in broods of up to 15 young per mother. Male leaves the female when she starts to incubate eggs. Orphans are accepted by other merganser mothers with young.

in flight

juvenile

SUMMER

Arctic Tern
Sterna paradisaea

Size: 12" (30 cm)

Male: A white and gray tern with a black cap and small dark red bill. Short red legs. Forked tail, seen in flight. Non-breeding plumage has an incomplete black cap and black bill.

Female: same as male

Juvenile: similar to non-breeding plumage, scattered brown overall

Nest: ground; female and male construct; 1 brood per year

Eggs: 2; olive with brown markings

Incubation: 20-24 days; female and male incubate

Fledging: 21-28 days; male and female feed young

Migration: complete, to South America

Food: small fish, aquatic insects, insects

Compare: Smaller than the breeding Bonaparte's Gull (pg. 341), which has a black head, black tail and tips of wings. Look for Arctic Tern's forked tail to help identify in flight.

Stan's Notes: Catches small fish by diving headfirst in water. Nests in large colonies with other tern species. While most nesting occurs in Alaska and the Northwest Territories of Canada, it also nests as far south as Maine. Returns to same nest site every year. Vigorously defends nest site and young from predators and people. Long-term relationship between mates. Young remain with the adults during migration to South America.

breeding
pg. 153

winter

YEAR-ROUND

White-tailed Ptarmigan
Lagopus leucura

Size: 12½" (32 cm)

Male: Winter plumage (Oct-Apr) is entirely white. Small dark bill.

Female: same as winter male

Juvenile: similar to breeding female, white on wings

Nest: ground; female builds; 1 brood per year

Eggs: 4-8; tan with brown markings

Incubation: 22-24 days; female incubates

Fledging: 10-15 days; female shows young what to eat

Migration: non-migrator to partial; will move around in winter to find food

Food: leaf and flower buds, seeds, insects, berries

Compare: The winter Willow Ptarmigan (pg. 339) has black sides on its tail. The winter male Rock Ptarmigan (pg. 337) has a black eye line.

Stan's Notes: Alone or in small unisex flocks in winter. Ptarmigans molt three times each year; other birds molt twice. In late autumn, molts to an all-white plumage that blends with winter landscapes. Moves to lower elevations during winter. Late summer plumage (Jul-Oct) is gray with rust and black spotting. When courting, male displays swollen red combs and alternates the pace of strutting, fast with slow. Female builds a shallow nest in spring, usually under a shrub, and lines it with fine grass, lichens and feathers. She delays nesting until fully molted into her summer camouflage plumage. If threatened at the nest, the female will perform a distraction display that includes hissing and clucking. Male leaves female shortly after eggs hatch. Species name *leucura* is Greek and means "white tail." Other ptarmigans have black-sided tails.

breeding
pg. 155

winter male

YEAR-ROUND

Rock Ptarmigan
Lagopus muta

Size: 14" (36 cm)

Male: Winter (Oct-Apr) is all white except for a black eye line and a black-sided tail, seen in flight. Small dark bill.

Female: all white, small dark bill, lacks eye lines

Juvenile: similar to breeding female, white outermost flight feathers

Nest: ground; female builds; 1 brood per year

Eggs: 6-9; tan with brown markings

Incubation: 21-24 days; female incubates

Fledging: 12-20 days; female shows young what to eat

Migration: non-migrator to partial; will move around in winter to find food

Food: leaf and flower buds, seeds, insects, berries

Compare: The winter Willow Ptarmigan (pg. 339) has a thicker bill than the winter female Rock Ptarmigan. Winter White-tailed Ptarmigan (pg. 335) lacks eye lines and black on tail.

Stan's Notes: Solitary or in small unisex flocks in winter, moving to lower elevations. All ptarmigans molt three times each year; most other birds molt twice. Molts in late autumn to white plumage and blends into winter landscapes. Molts in late winter into breeding plumage. Courting male (Apr-Jun) is mostly white with bright red combs and a dirty yellow and tan chest. Male displays his red combs to female. Female builds a shallow ground nest, often among rocks, and covers it with vegetation until clutch is complete. Male leaves female when she starts to incubate. Common name comes from its habitat on rocky tundra. Latin species name *muta* means "animal that can only mutter or has a weak call" and refers to its quiet call.

winter

breeding
pg. 157

YEAR-ROUND

Willow Ptarmigan
Lagopus lagopus

Size: 14" (36 cm)

Male: Winter plumage (Oct-Apr) is entirely white with a stout black bill. Black edges on tail, seen in flight.

Female: same as winter male

Juvenile: similar to breeding female, white on wings

Nest: ground; female builds; 1 brood per year

Eggs: 5-14; blackish brown with cream markings

Incubation: 21-23 days; female incubates

Fledging: 10-14 days; female shows young what to eat

Migration: non-migrator to partial; will move around in winter to find food

Food: buds (mainly willow), seeds, insects

Compare: Winter White-tailed Ptarmigan (pg. 335) lacks black edges on tail. The winter male Rock Ptarmigan (pg. 337) has a black stripe through its eyes.

Stan's Notes: "Ptarmigan" comes from a Gaelic word for this kind of bird, *tarmachan*. Common name comes from its favor for willow buds and leaves. All ptarmigans molt three times each year; most other birds molt twice. Molts to white plumage in late autumn that blends in with the winter landscape. Moves to lower elevations in winter. During spring, female molts to a camouflage coloration that enables her to blend in with landscape while she incubates. Builds nest on the open tundra; lines its nest with leaves, grass and a few feathers. Unlike other ptarmigan species, the male remains with the female to raise young. However, females without mates are just as successful rearing their young as the females with mates.

non-breeding

in flight

breeding

MIGRATION
SUMMER

Bonaparte's Gull
Larus philadelphia

Size: 14" (36 cm); up to 3-foot wingspan

Male: A mostly white gull during breeding season (Apr-Aug) with gray upper surface of wings and back. Black head, small black bill and a white crescent marking around each eye. Black wing tips and tail, seen in flight. Non-breeding adult lacks a black head and has a dark ear spot.

Female: same as male

Juvenile: similar to non-breeding male

Nest: platform; female and male construct; 1-2 broods per year

Eggs: 2-4; light brown with brown markings

Incubation: 20-24 days; female and male incubate

Fledging: 21-25 days; female and male feed young

Migration: complete, to coastal California and Mexico

Food: aquatic and terrestrial insects, fish

Compare: Larger than Arctic Tern (pg. 333), which has a black cap unlike the black head of the breeding Bonaparte's Gull. Look for a small black bill to help identify Bonaparte's Gull.

Stan's Notes: Rarely with other gull species, presumably due to its small size. Said to resemble a tern species because of its small size, short thin bill and swift flight. Seen on lakes and rivers in summer and during migration. Nests in half of Alaska where there is water. Builds its own nest or takes an abandoned nest in a tree, mainly conifers. Takes two years for young to obtain adult plumage.

breeding

winter

in flight

Mew Gull
Larus canus

Size: 16" (40 cm); up to 3½-foot wingspan

Male: White gull with dark gray back and wings. Black wing tips. Red ring around dark eyes. Yellow legs. Breeding has a small unmarked yellow bill. Winter plumage has a brown-streaked head and neck. Yellow bill with a dark ring around the tip.

Female: same as male

Juvenile: gray to brown overall with a black-tipped yellow bill

Nest: ground; female and male construct; 1 brood per year

Eggs: 2-3; brown with brown markings

Incubation: 24-26 days; female and male incubate

Fledging: 30-32 days; female and male feed young

Migration: complete, to western coastal U.S., Mexico

Food: insects, fish, shellfish, fruit

Compare: Much smaller than Herring Gull (pg. 347) and Glaucous-winged Gull (pg. 349). Look for the tiny yellow bill and diminutive size.

Stan's Notes: Small gull with a remarkably small bill. A common summer resident in most of Alaska. Usually seen with other gulls. Often drops sea urchins from heights to crack open and eat. This is a three-year gull, taking three years to reach maturity. Starts out entirely light brown. With a brown-streaked head and neck, the second-year gull resembles the winter adult. Third-year gull has breeding plumage. The young return to their natal colony to nest. Known in Europe as Common Gull.

Snowy Owl
Bubo scandiacus

Size: 23" (58 cm); up to 4-foot wingspan

Male: All white with a relatively small round head, bright yellow eyes and small dark bill. Feet are completely covered with white feathers.

Female: same as male, but dark bars overall

Juvenile: gray with a white face (gray changes later to white), covered with dark horizontal bars, the younger the bird, the more barring

Nest: ground, often in gravel or atop a hummock; 1 brood per year

Eggs: 3-4; white without markings

Incubation: 32-34 days; female incubates

Fledging: 14-20 days; male and female feed young

Migration: partial to non-migrator, irruptive, to Alaska, Canada and northern states

Food: mammals, birds

Compare: Our only white owl, rarely confused with any other bird.

Stan's Notes: A nesting bird in parts of coastal Alaska, known for feeding on lemmings. Moves down through the state in winter in search of food when lemmings aren't plentiful. In some years, may move as far south as northern Texas. The clutch size is dependent on the availability of prey. Prefers to rest on the ground. Male feeds incubating female, but does not incubate. Young hatch several days apart (asynchronously). Families remain together until fall. Often seen on frozen lakes or bays in winter. Blends in with snow. Flies low to the ground on relatively narrow wings with full, stiff wing beats. Shy and unapproachable, unlike many other owls.

in flight

breeding

winter

juvenile

SUMMER
WINTER

Herring Gull
Larus argentatus

Size: 23-26" (58-66 cm); up to 5-foot wingspan

Male: Snow-white bird with slate gray wings and black wing tips with tiny white spots. Bill is yellow with an orange-red spot near the tip of lower bill. Pinkish legs. Winter plumage head and neck are dirty gray to brown.

Female: same as male

Juvenile: uniformly mottled brown to gray, black bill

Nest: ground; female and male construct; 1 brood per year

Eggs: 2-3; olive with brown markings

Incubation: 24-28 days; female and male incubate

Fledging: 35-36 days; female and male feed young

Migration: complete, to southern coastal Alaska, western states and Mexico

Food: fish, insects, clams, eggs, baby birds

Compare: Glaucous-winged Gull (pg. 349) is similar, but has gray wing tips with white spots. Glaucous Gull (pg. 351) is also similar, but has unmarked white wing tips.

Stan's Notes: A common gull of large lakes. An opportunistic bird, scavenging for food from dumpsters, but will also take other birds' eggs and young right from the nest. Often drops clams and other shellfish from heights to break shells and get to the soft interior. Nests in colonies, returning to the same site year after year. Lines its ground nest with grasses and seaweed. Takes about four years for juveniles to obtain adult plumage. Adults molt to dirty gray in winter and look similar to juveniles.

winter

in flight

breeding

Glaucous-winged Gull
Larus glaucescens

Size: 26" (66 cm); up to 4¾-foot wingspan

Male: White gull with a light gray back and wings, with white spots on wing tips. Yellow bill with red spot on the lower bill. Dark eyes with a pink eye-ring around each eye. Pink legs. Winter plumage has a brown-streaked head and neck.

Female: same as male

Juvenile: gray to brown overall with a black bill

Nest: ground; female and male construct; 1 brood per year

Eggs: 1-3; olive with brown markings

Incubation: 27-29 days; female and male incubate

Fledging: 35-55 days; female and male feed young

Migration: partial to non-migrator in Alaska

Food: insects, fish, shellfish, garbage

Compare: Glaucous Gull (pg. 351) is nearly identical, but has a yellow eye-ring around each eye and unmarked white wing tips.

Stan's Notes: A four-year gull, taking four years to reach maturity. Starts out entirely gray to brown. Second-year gull is light gray with patches of white. Third-year gull resembles the winter adult, with a brown-streaked head and neck, white body and gray back and wings. Fourth-year gull has breeding plumage. Returns to the same nesting colony each year, often breeding with mate from previous year. Male bends forward and pops head up while calling for mate. Hybridizes with Glaucous Gulls and Herring Gulls.

winter

in flight

breeding

Glaucous Gull
Larus hyperboreus

YEAR-ROUND
SUMMER
WINTER

Size: 27" (69 cm); up to 5-foot wingspan

Male: Breeding (Mar-Sep) plumage is white with a light gray back and upper surface of wings. Unmarked white wing tips. Yellow eye-ring around each eye. Yellow bill with a red spot on lower bill. Winter (Sep-Apr) has brown streaks on head and nape.

Female: same as male

Juvenile: overall light brown with a black-tipped bill

Nest: ground; female and male construct; 1 brood per year

Eggs: 2-4; olive with brown markings

Incubation: 27-28 days; female and male incubate

Fledging: 45-50 days; female and male feed young

Migration: complete to non-migrator, to the southern coast of Alaska

Food: small fish, aquatic insects, carrion, bird eggs

Compare: Nearly identical to Glaucous-winged Gull (pg. 349), which has gray wing tips with white spots and pink eye-rings.

Stan's Notes: One of the largest and palest of our gulls. A four-year gull that starts out light brown with a black-tipped bill. Second-year gull is nearly all white. Third-year gull has a gray back and upper wing surface with brown streaks on head and nape of neck. Attains breeding plumage in the fourth year. Nests in large colonies, often with other species, on rocky coasts, islands and tundra lakes. Constructs a large mound of soft grass and other plant material and usually lines it with feathers. Uses the same nest for many years.

white
morph

blue morph

juvenile

in flight

MIGRATION

Snow Goose
Chen caerulescens

Size: 25-38" (63-96 cm); up to 4½-foot wingspan

Male: A mostly white goose with varying patches of black and brown. Black wing tips. Pink bill and legs. Some individuals are grayish with a white head.

Female: same as male

Juvenile: overall dull gray with a dark bill

Nest: ground; female builds; 1 brood per year

Eggs: 3-5; white without markings

Incubation: 23-25 days; female incubates

Fledging: 45-49 days; female and male teach young to feed

Migration: complete, to southwestern states, Mexico

Food: aquatic insects and plants

Compare: The Tundra Swan (pg. 355) and Trumpeter Swan (pg. 357) lack black wing tips. The Canada Goose (pg. 303) has a black neck and white chin strap.

Stan's Notes: Two color morphs. The more common white morph is pure white with black wing tips. Gray morph is often called blue, with a white head, gray chest and back and pink bill and legs. Thick serrated bill for pulling up plants. Breeds in large colonies on the northern Canadian tundra. Females begin breeding at 2-3 years. Older females produce more eggs and are more successful than the younger females. Seen by the thousands during migration, usually with Sandhill Cranes.

juvenile

in flight

Tundra Swan
Cygnus columbianus

Size: 50-54" (127-137 cm); up to 5½-ft. wingspan

Male: A large all-white swan. Black bill, legs and feet. Small yellow mark in front of each eye.

Female: same as male

Juvenile: same size as adult, gray plumage, pinkish gray bill

Nest: ground; female and male construct; 1 brood per year

Eggs: 4-5; creamy white without markings

Incubation: 35-40 days; female and male incubate

Fledging: 60-70 days; female and male feed young

Migration: complete, to West and East coast states

Food: plants, aquatic insects

Compare: The Trumpeter Swan (pg. 357) is larger and lacks yellow marks on its face. Snow Goose (pg. 353) is much smaller and has black wing tips. Look for Tundra Swan's black bill and legs.

Stan's Notes: Nests on the tundra of Alaska, hence its common name. During migration, gathers in large numbers in some lakes and rivers to rest, frequently staying until the water freezes before continuing on. Flies in large V-shaped wedges. Often seen in large family groups consisting of 20 or more individuals. The young are easy to distinguish by their gray plumage and pinkish bills. Gives a high-pitched, whistle-like call.

in flight

juvenile

MIGRATION
SUMMER

Trumpeter Swan
Cygnus buccinator

Size: 60" (152 cm); up to 6½-foot wingspan

Male: A large all-white swan with an all-black bill, legs and feet.

Female: same as male

Juvenile: same size as adult, gray plumage, pinkish gray bill

Nest: ground; female and male construct; 1 brood per year

Eggs: 4-6; creamy white without markings

Incubation: 33-37 days; female incubates

Fledging: 100-120 days; female and male feed young

Migration: complete, to coastal Canada and West coast states

Food: aquatic plants, insects

Compare: Very similar to the Tundra Swan (pg. 355), which is smaller and has a small yellow mark in front of each eye. The Snow Goose (pg. 353) is much smaller than Trumpeter Swan and has black wing tips.

Stan's Notes: Was once hunted to near extinction, but has been reintroduced with great success in many parts of its former range. Most breeding programs were started with eggs taken from Alaskan swans. Frequently seen with large colored neck or wing tags, which identify reintroduced individuals. Holds neck with a slight bend or kink at the base. Pairs defend large territories and construct large mound nests at the edge of water. Common name comes from its trumpet-like call.

female

male

SUMMER

Wilson's Warbler
Wilsonia pusilla

Size: 4¾" (12 cm)

Male: Dull yellow upper and bright yellow lower. Distinctive black cap. Large black eyes and small thin bill.

Female: same as male, but lacking the black cap

Juvenile: similar to female

Nest: cup; female builds; 1 brood per year

Eggs: 4-6; white with brown markings

Incubation: 10-13 days; female incubates

Fledging: 8-11 days; female and male feed young

Migration: complete, to coastal Texas, Mexico and Central America

Food: insects

Compare: The Orange-crowned Warbler (pg. 361) is paler yellow and lacks the black cap of the male Wilson's Warbler. The Eastern Yellow Wagtail (pg. 365) is larger, has white eye brows and lacks male Wilson's black cap.

Stan's Notes: A widespread warbler of low to mid-level elevations Can be found near water in willow and alder thickets. Its all-insect diet makes it one of the top insect-eating birds in North America. Often flicks its tail and spreads its wings when hopping among thick shrubs, looking for insects. The females often mate with males that have the best territories and that might already have mates (polygyny).

SUMMER

Orange-crowned Warbler
Vermivora celata

Size: 5" (13 cm)

Male: An overall pale yellow bird with a dark line through eyes. Faint streaking on sides and chest. Small thin bill. Tawny orange crown, often invisible.

Female: same as male, but very slightly duller, often indistinguishable in the field

Juvenile: same as adults

Nest: cup; female builds; 1-2 broods per year

Eggs: 3-6; white with brown markings

Incubation: 12-14 days; female incubates

Fledging: 8-10 days; female and male feed young

Migration: complete, to coastal California, Mexico and Central America

Food: insects, fruit, nectar

Compare: Male Wilson's Warbler (pg. 359) is brighter yellow with a distinctive black cap. Yellow Warbler (pg. 363) is darker yellow than the pale yellow of the Orange-crowned.

Stan's Notes: A nesting resident in most of Alaska but often seen more during migration, when large groups move together. Builds a bulky, well-concealed nest on the ground with nest rim at ground level. Known to drink flower nectar. The orange crown tends to be hidden and is rarely seen in the field. A widespread breeder, from Alaska to across Canada and south to California and western Texas.

male

female

SUMMER

Yellow Warbler
Dendroica petechia

Size: 5" (13 cm)

Male: Yellow warbler with orange streaks on the chest and belly. Long, pointed dark bill.

Female: same as male, but lacking orange streaking

Juvenile: similar to female, only much duller

Nest: cup; female builds; 1 brood per year

Eggs: 4-5; white with brown markings

Incubation: 11-12 days; female incubates

Fledging: 10-12 days; female and male feed young

Migration: complete, to southwestern states, Mexico, Central and South America

Food: insects

Compare: Look for the orange streaking on the chest of the male. The Orange-crowned Warbler (pg. 361) is paler yellow. Yellow-rumped Warbler (pg. 239) has only spots of yellow unlike the orange streaking on the chest of the male Yellow Warbler.

Stan's Notes: A common warbler throughout most of Alaska. Seen in gardens and shrubby areas near water. It is a prolific insect eater, gleaning small caterpillars and other insects from tree leaves. Male is often seen higher up in trees than the female. The female is less conspicuous. Starts to migrate in August and returns in late April. Males arrive 1-2 weeks before females to claim territories. Migrates at night in mixed flocks of warblers. Rests and feeds during the day.

Eastern Yellow Wagtail
Motacilla tschutschensis

Size: 6½" (16 cm)

Male: Yellow chest and belly. Head and back are dull yellow to olive green. White chin. Dark cheek patches. Narrow white eyebrows.

Female: similar to male

Juvenile: overall gray with a dark border around a white throat

Nest: cup; female builds; 1 brood per year

Eggs: 4-7; pale white with brown markings

Incubation: 10-14 days; female and male incubate

Fledging: 14-16 days; female and male feed young

Migration: complete, to the East Indies, China, Asia and southern North Africa

Food: insects, snails, berries, worms

Compare: Larger than the male Northern Wheatear (pg. 243), which has a black mask and wings. Male Wilson's Warbler (pg. 359) is smaller, has a black cap and lacks the white eyebrows of Eastern Yellow Wagtail.

Stan's Notes: Named for the continuous up and down motion of its tail. Nests beneath an overhanging bank or next to a clump of plants (tussock). Builds nest from grass and leaves and lines it with hair and feathers. Male performs a courtship flight of up to 90 feet (27 m) and floats down on stiff cupped wings, singing slowly while spreading and elevating its tail. When close to ground, it glides to a perch or lands on the ground, then repeats flight and display. In North America, it is found only in Alaska. Migrates west to Eurasia, where it is widespread and very common.

female

male pg. 321

YEAR-ROUND

Red Crossbill
Loxia curvirostra

Size: 6½" (16 cm)

Female: A pale yellow-gray sparrow-sized bird with a pale yellow chest and light gray patch on the throat. Dark brown wings. Short dark brown tail. Long, pointed crossed bill.

Male: dirty red to orange with a bright red crown and rump, dark brown wings, a short dark brown tail and a crossed bill

Juvenile: streaked with tinges of yellow, bill gradually crosses about 2 weeks after fledging

Nest: cup; female builds; 1 brood per year

Eggs: 3-4; bluish white with brown markings

Incubation: 14-18 days; female incubates

Fledging: 16-20 days; female and male feed young

Migration: irruptive; moves around Alaska in winter to find food, will wander as far as Mexico

Food: seeds, leaf buds, comes to seed feeders

Compare: Female White-winged Crossbill (pg. 369) has white wing bars. Female Pine Grosbeak (pg. 263) lacks the crossed bill.

Stan's Notes: The long crossed bill is adapted for extracting seeds from pine and spruce cones, its favorite food. Often dangles upside down like a parrot to reach cones. Also seen on the ground where it eats grit, which helps digest food. Nests in coniferous forests. Some studies show up to nine distinct populations of Red Crossbills, but they are nearly impossible to distinguish in the field. Plumage can be highly variable among individuals. Irruptive behavior makes it more common in some winters and nonexistent in others.

male pg. 323

White-winged Crossbill
Loxia leucoptera

Size: 6½" (16 cm)

Female: Sparrow-sized bird with a pale yellow breast covered with indistinct streaks. Dark wings. Two large white wing bars. Dark tail. Long, slender crossed bill.

Male: red-to-pink bird, black wings and tail, 2 large white wing bars, gray sides and lower belly, a long, slender crossed bill with a dark spot at base (lore)

Juvenile: similar to female

Nest: cup; female builds; 1 brood per year

Eggs: 3-5; pale blue with brown markings

Incubation: 12-14 days; female incubates

Fledging: 16-20 days; female and male feed young

Migration: non-migrator to irruptive; moves around in winter to find food

Food: seeds, berries, insects; comes to seed feeders

Compare: The female Red Crossbill (pg. 367) is very similar to female White-winged Crossbill, but lacks the white wing bars. The female Pine Grosbeak (pg. 263) is much larger and lacks the crossed bill.

Stan's Notes: This bird dangles upside down to reach pine and spruce cones, using its long crossed bill to extracts the seeds. Eats berries and insects to a lesser extent. Usually seen on the ground picking up grit, which helps grind the seeds. Moves around to find a plentiful supply of seeds. Plumage can be highly variable among individuals, with older males more colorful than the younger ones.

HELPFUL RESOURCES

Birder's Bug Book, The. Waldbauer, Gilbert. Cambridge: Harvard University Press, 1998.

Birder's Dictionary. Cox, Randall T. Helena, MT: Falcon Press Publishing, 1996.

Birder's Handbook, The. Ehrlich, Paul R., David S. Dobkin and Darryl Wheye. New York: Simon and Schuster, 1988.

Birds Do It, Too: The Amazing Sex Life of Birds. Harrison, Kit and George H. Harrison. Minocqua, WI: Willow Creek Press, 1997.

Birds of Forest, Yard, and Thicket. Eastman, John. Mechanicsburg, PA: Stackpole Books, 1997.

Birds of North America. Kaufman, Kenn. New York: Houghton Mifflin, 2000.

Blackbirds of the Americas. Orians, Gordon H. Seattle: University of Washington Press, 1985.

Cry of the Sandhill Crane, The. Grooms, Steve. Minocqua, WI: NorthWord Press, 1992.

Dictionary of American Bird Names, The. Choate, Ernest A. Boston: Harvard Common Press, 1985.

Dictionary of Birds of the United States. Holloway, Joel E. Portland, OR: Timber Press, 2003.

Everything You Never Learned About Birds. Rupp, Rebecca. Pownal, VT: Storey Publishing, 1997.

Field Guide to the Birds of North America: Third Edition. Washington, DC: National Geographic Society, 1999.

Field Guide to Warblers of North America, A. Dunn, Jon and Kimball Garrett. Boston: Houghton Mifflin, 1997.

Field Guide to Western Birds, A. Peterson, Roger Tory. Boston: Houghton Mifflin, 1998.

Folklore of Birds. Martin, Laura C. Old Saybrook, CT: Globe Pequot Press, 1996.

Guide to Bird Behavior, A: Vol I, II, III. Stokes, Donald and Lillian Stokes. Boston: Little, Brown and Company, 1989.

How Birds Migrate. Kerlinger, Paul. Mechanicsburg, PA: Stackpole Books, 1995.

Lives of Birds, The: Birds of the World and Their Behavior. Short, Lester L. Collingdale, PA: DIANE Publishing, 2000.

Lives of North American Birds. Kaufman, Kenn. Boston: Houghton Mifflin, 1996.

Living on the Wind. Weidensaul, Scott. New York: North Point Press, 2000.

National Audubon Society: North American Birdfeeder Handbook. Burton, Robert. New York: Dorling Kindersley Publishing, 1995.

National Audubon Society: The Sibley Guide to Bird Life and Behavior. Edited by David Allen Sibley, Chris Elphick and John B. Dunning, Jr. New York: Alfred A. Knopf, 2001.

National Audubon Society: The Sibley Guide to Birds. Sibley, David Allen. New York: Alfred A. Knopf, 2000.

Photographic Guide to North American Raptors, A. Wheeler, Brian K. and William S. Clark. New York: Academic Press, 1999.

Raptors of Western North America: The Wheeler Guides. Wheeler, Brian K. Princeton, NJ: Princeton University Press, 2003.

Secret Lives of Birds, The. Gingras, Pierre. Toronto: Key Porter Books, 1997.

Secrets of the Nest. Dunning, Joan. Boston: Houghton Mifflin, 1994.

Sparrows and Buntings: A Guide to the Sparrows and Buntings of North America and the World. Byers, Clive, Jon Curson and Urban Olsson. New York: Houghton Mifflin, 1995.

Stokes Bluebird Book: The Complete Guide to Attracting Bluebirds. Stokes, Donald and Lillian Stokes. Boston: Little, Brown and Company, 1991.

Stokes Field Guide to Birds: Western Region. Stokes, Donald and Lillian Stokes. Boston: Little, Brown and Company, 1996.

Alaska Birding Hotlines

To report unusual bird sightings or possibly hear recordings of where birds have been seen, you can often call pre-recorded hotlines detailing such information. Since these hotlines are usually staffed by volunteers, and phone numbers and even the organizations that host them often change, the phone numbers are not listed here. To obtain the numbers, go to your favorite internet search engine, type in something like "rare bird alert hotline Alaska" and follow the links provided.

Web Pages

The internet is a valuable place to learn more about birds. You may find birding on the net a fun way to discover additional information or to spend a long winter night. These web sites will assist you in your pursuit of birds. If a web address doesn't work (they often change a bit), just enter the name of the group into a search engine to track down the new web address.

Site	Address
Alaska Department of Fish and Game	www.adfg.state.ak.us
American Birding Association	www.americanbirding.org
Cornell Lab of Ornithology	www.birds.cornell.edu
Author Stan Tekiela's home page	www.naturesmart.com

CHECK LIST/INDEX BY SPECIES

Use the boxes to check the birds you've seen.

ABOUT THE AUTHOR

Stan Tekiela is a naturalist, author and wildlife photographer with a Bachelor of Science degree in Natural History from the University of Minnesota. He has been a professional naturalist for more than 20 years and is a member of the Minnesota Naturalist Association, Minnesota Ornithologist Union, Outdoor Writers Association of America, North American Nature Photography Association and Canon Professional Services. Stan actively studies and photographs birds throughout the United States. He has received various national and regional awards for outdoor education and writing. A columnist and radio person-ality, his syndicated column appears in over 20 cities and he can be heard on a number of radio stations. Stan resides in Victoria, Minnesota, with wife Katherine and daughter Abigail. He can be contacted via his web page at www.naturesmart.com.

Stan authors field guides for other states including guides for birds, birds of prey, mammals, reptiles and amphibians, trees and wildflowers.